SOCIAL STATISTICS AND THE CITY

David M. Heer, Editor

Report of a Conference held in
Washington, D.C., June 22-23, 1967

FOREWORD


At one point in the course of the 1950's John Kenneth Galbraith
observed that it is the statisticians, as much as any single group,
who shape public policy, for the simple reason that societies never
really become effectively concerned with social problems until they
learn to measure them.  An unassuming truth, perhaps, but a mighty
one, and one that did more than he may know to sustain morale in a
number of Washington bureaucracies (hateful word!) during a period
when the relevant cabinet officers had on their own reached very much
the same conclusion—and distrusted their charges all the more in consequence.  For it is one of the ironies of American government that
individuals and groups that have been most resistant to liberal social
change have quite accurately perceived that social statistics are all
too readily transformed into political dynamite, whilst in a curious
way the reform temperament has tended to view the whole statistical
process as plodding, overcautious, and somehow a brake on progress.
(Why must every statistic be accompanied by detailed notes about the
size of the "standard error"?)

The answer, of course, is that this is what must be done if the
fact is to be accurately stated, and ultimately accepted.  But, given
this atmosphere of suspicion on the one hand and impatience on the

other, it is something of a wonder that the statistical officers of the federal government have with such fortitude and fairness remained faithful to a high intellectual calling, and an even more demanding public trust.

There is no agency of which this is more true than the Bureau of the Census, the first, and still the most important, information-gathering agency of the federal government. For getting on, now, for two centuries, the Census has collected and compiled the essential facts of the American experience. Of late the ten-year cycle has begun to modulate somewhat, and as more and more current reports have been forthcoming, the Census has been quietly transforming itself into a continuously flowing source of information about the American people. In turn, American society has become more and more dependent on it. It would be difficult to find an aspect of public or private life not touched and somehow shaped by Census information. And yet for all this, it is somehow ignored. To declare that the Census is without friends would be absurd. But partisans? When Census appropriations are cut, who bleeds on Capitol Hill or in the Executive Office of the President? The answer is almost everyone in general, and therefore no one in particular. But the result, too often, is the neglect, even the abuse, of an indispensable public institution, which often of late has served better than it has been served.

The papers in this collection, as Professor Heer's introduction explains, were presented at a conference held in June 1967 with the avowed purpose of arousing a measure of public concern about the difficulties encountered by the Census in obtaining a full count of the urban poor, especially perhaps the Negro poor.  It became apparent, for example, that in 1960 one fifth of nonwhite males aged 25-29 had in effect disappeared and had been left out of the Census count altogether.  Invisible men.  Altogether, one tenth of the nonwhite population had been "missed."  The ramifications of this fact were considerable, and its implications will suggest themselves immediately.  It was hoped that a public airing of the issue might lead to greater public support to ensure that the Census would have the resources in 1970 to do what is, after all, its fundamental job, that of counting all the American people.  As the reader will see, the scholarly case for providing this support was made with considerable energy and candor.  But perhaps the most compelling argument arose from a chance remark by a conference participant to the effect that if the decennial census were not required by the Constitution, the Bureau would doubtless never have survived the economy drives of the nineteenth century.  The thought flashed:  the full enumeration of the American population is not simply an optional public service provided by government for the use of sales managers, sociologists, and regional planners.  It is, rather, the constitutionally mandated process whereby political representation in the Congress is distributed as between different areas of the nation.  It is a matter not of convenience but of the highest seriousness, affecting the very foundations of sovereignty.  That being the case, there is no lawful course but to provide the Bureau with whatever resources are necessary to obtain a full enumeration.  Inasmuch as

Negroes and other "minorities" are concentrated in specific urban locations, to undercount significantly the population in those areas is to deny residents their rights under Article I, Section 3 of the Constitution, as well, no doubt, as under Section 1 of the Fourteenth Amendment. Given the further, more recent practice of distributing federal, state, and local categorical aid on the basis not only of the number but also social and economic characteristics of local populations, the constitutional case for full enumeration would seem to be further strengthened.

A sound legal case? Others will judge; and possibly one day the courts will decide. But of one thing the conference had no doubt: the common-sense case is irrefutable. America needs to count all its people. (And reciprocally, all its people need to make themselves available to be counted.) But if the legal case adds any strength to the common-sense argument, it remains only to add that should either of the arguments bring some improvement in the future, it will be but another instance of the generosity of the Carnegie Corporation, which provided funds for the conference and for this publication.

Daniel P. Moynihan, Director<br>Joint Center for Urban Studies

Cambridge, Massachusetts
February 1968

C O N T E N T S

FOREWORD:  Daniel P. Moynihan                                          iii

INTRODUCTION:  David M. Heer                                             1

1.  Completeness of Coverage of the Nonwhite Population in the          13
    1960 Census and Current Estimates, and Some Implications

            Jacob S. Siegel


2.  Procedural Difficulties in Taking Past Censuses in Pre-             55
    dominantly Negro, Puerto Rican, and Mexican Areas

            Leon Pritzker and N. D. Rothwell


3.  Needed Innovations in 1970 Census Data Collection Proce-            80
    dures:  A Census View

            Conrad Taeuber


4.  Needed Improvements in Census Data Collection Procedures            91
    with Special Reference to the Disadvantaged

            Everett S. Lee


5.  Vital Statistics for the Negro, Puerto Rican, and Mexican          100
    Populations:  Present Quality and Plans for Improvement

            Robert D. Grove


6.  Needed Statistics for Minority Groups in Metropolitan Areas        118

            Daniel O. Price


APPENDIX:  An Evaluation of Coverage in the 1960 Census of             132
           Population by Techniques of Demographic Analysis
           and by Composite Methods

            Jacob S. Siegel and Melvin Zelnik


RESOLUTIONS OF THE CONFERENCE                                          174


LIST OF CONFERENCE PARTICIPANTS                                        183

# INTRODUCTION

As far back as 1955 a leading American demographer demonstrated that a substantial proportion of the Negro population had not been counted in the 1950 Census.[1] According to Ansley J. Coale's estimate, 11 percent of all nonwhites in the United States were not enumerated at that time. However, Coale's work received little attention outside the community of professional demographers. After the 1960 Census, additional work was undertaken to estimate the degree of underenumeration of the nonwhite population.[2] At this time, however, the climate was more favorable to a wider dissemination of the findings. During the previous decade social scientists had paid relatively little attention to the American Negro, but in the early 1960's interest had mounted rapidly.

---

[1] Ansley J. Coale, "The Population of the United States in 1950 Classified by Age, Sex, and Color—A Revision of Census Figures," Journal of the American Statistical Association, Vol. 50, No. 1 (March 1955), pp. 16-54.

[2] Donald J. Bogue, Bhaskar D. Misra, and D. P. Dandekar, "A New Estimate of the Negro Population and Negro Vital Rates in the United States, 1930-1960," Demography, Vol. 1, No. 1 (1964), pp. 339-358; U. S. Bureau of the Census, "Estimates of the Population of the United States and Components of Change, by Age, Color, and Sex, 1950 to 1960," Current Population Reports, Series P-25, No. 310, by J. S. Siegel, D. S. Akers, and W. D. Jones (June 30, 1965); and Jacob S. Siegel and Melvin Zelnik, "An Evaluation of Coverage in the Census of Population by Techniques of Demographic Analysis and by Composite Methods," Proceedings of the Social Statistics Section, 1966, American Statistical Association, pp. 71-85.

Daniel P. Moynihan, then Assistant Secretary of Labor, became aware of the findings concerning the underenumeration of nonwhites in the census while preparing his now famous report The Negro Family: The Case for National Action, which was published in 1965.[3] In the fall of 1966 Moynihan became director of the Joint Center for Urban Studies of the Massachusetts Institute of Technology and Harvard University. In December of that year he asked me if I would plan a conference that would (1) publicize the fact that many Negroes had not been counted in the 1960 Census and (2) attempt to arouse national concern about the matter. In further discussion we decided that the proposed conference should be broadened to include not only census underenumeration of Negroes but the adequacy of all official social statistics for Negroes, Puerto Ricans, and Mexicans in the United States. In January 1967 the Carnegie Corporation of New York informed us that it was willing to provide financial support for the conference.

A prime aim of the conference was to stimulate public interest in the importance of social statistics for Negroes, Puerto Ricans, and Mexicans so that the chief agencies concerned with gathering such statistics—the U. S. Bureau of the Census and the National Center for Health Statistics—might obtain a more adequate budget from Congress to improve the quality and quantity of data for these groups. With this goal in mind we decided that the conference would have to be held before the fall of 1967, since the Bureau of the Budget was to decide upon the recommended appropriations for the 1970 Decennial Census

---

[3]Washington, D. C.: Government Printing Office, 1965.

at that time. The final dates established were June 22 and 23, 1967, and the conference was to be held in Washington, D. C.

Among those providing invaluable assistance in planning the conference were Dr. A. Ross Eckler, Director of the U. S. Bureau of the Census; Dr. Conrad Taeuber, Assistant Director for Demographic Fields, U. S. Bureau of the Census; and Dr. Anders Lunde, Assistant Director of the Division of Vital Statistics, National Center for Health Statistics, U. S. Public Health Service. It was decided that six papers should be presented on the first day of the conference. On the morning of the second day the participants would divide into three workshops to discuss recommendations with respect to each of the following topics: (1) ways of improving coverage of Negroes, Puerto Ricans, and Mexicans in the census, (2) ways of improving vital statistics for these groups, and (3) needed additions in available social statistics for the three groups. On the afternoon of the second day, the rapporteurs from each of the morning sessions would report the recommendations of their respective panels, and the conference as a whole would then adopt a general series of recommendations.

The first paper of the conference was delivered by Jacob Siegel, Staff Assistant, Population Division, U. S. Bureau of the Census, and was entitled "Completeness of Coverage of the Nonwhite Population in the 1960 Census and Current Estimates, and Some Implications." Siegel focused attention on the nonwhite rather than the Negro population because of his lack of information specifically for the Negro group. However, this change was immaterial since Negroes constitute over 90 percent of the nonwhite population. Furthermore, Siegel was not able to consider census underenumeration of Puerto Ricans or Mexicans because of lack of available data.

A principal contribution of Siegel's paper was his estimate of the net understatement of the white and nonwhite groups in both the 1960 and the 1950 Censuses. With respect to 1960 Siegel estimated that 2.2 percent of all white persons were not counted and 9.5 percent of all nonwhites. For the total population the net understatement was 3.1 percent. Nevertheless, the net understatement in the 1960 Census was not uniquely large. In fact Siegel believed that the net understatement in the 1960 Census was less than it had been in 1950. He estimated that in 1950 the net understatement for the entire population had been 3.6 percent, for the white population 2.6 percent, and for the nonwhite population 11.5 percent. In 1960 the net underenumeration for nonwhite males was larger (10.9 percent) than for nonwhite females (8.1 percent). Nonwhite males from 20 to 39 years old were particularly subject to undercount. Among this group 17 percent failed to be counted, or about one in every six.

Siegel also discussed the coverage of the nonwhite population in the Current Population Survey, a monthly survey of about 35,000 households which provides national data on employment, unemployment, and other population characteristics. Siegel estimated that the 1965 surveys missed 17 percent of nonwhite males 14 years old and over and 9 percent of nonwhite females of this age group. As with the decennial census, the largest proportion that failed to be counted was among young males: the figure was 25 percent among nonwhite males 20 to 39 years old.

Siegel also discussed the possible effect of failure to achieve a complete count of the nonwhite population on the accuracy of the reported characteristics for nonwhites. It is mathematically conceivable that these effects could be quite large. For example, consider a group of nonwhite males where 25 percent of those who should have been were not counted. Suppose that among those who were counted 10 percent reported that they were unemployed. Suppose, further, that all of those who were not counted were unemployed, then the true proportion unemployed in the total group would be 32.5 percent rather than 10 percent. However, as Siegel points out, the crucial fact is that we do not know what proportion of the uncounted were unemployed. If fewer of those not enumerated than of those enumerated were unemployed, then the true proportion unemployed could be less than 10 percent.

Siegel's paper made other important points. One of these concerned the effect of the underenumeration of nonwhites on the reported birth and death rates for this group. For example, although the reported birth rate for the nonwhite population of the United States in 1960 was 33.3 per thousand, the corrected rate is only 30.1 per thousand. Similarly, the reported death rate for nonwhites in 1960 was 9.6 per thousand, whereas the corrected rate was only 8.8. Siegel concluded his paper by warning that it is quite probable the distortion in data for nonwhites in many local areas is considerably worse than it is for the nation as a whole. This caveat is of particular importance to city planners, school officials, and other persons for whom the accuracy of local area data is of vital importance.

The second paper of the conference, "Procedural Difficulties in

Taking Past Censuses in Predominantly Negro, Puerto Rican, and Mexican Areas," was presented by Leon Pritzker and N. D. Rothwell, both of the Response Research Branch of the Statistical Research Division, U. S. Bureau of the Census. Pritzker and Rothwell pointed out that skepticism concerning completeness of the census count has existed for a long time. George Washington, for example, doubted the accuracy of the nation's first census taken in 1790. They noted that a person could fail to be enumerated in the census for one of two reasons: (1) he lived in a housing unit which the enumerator missed completely, or (2) the enumerator failed to count him although she counted the housing unit. Pritzker and Rothwell then cited evidence indicating that a large majority of white persons who failed to be counted lived in housing units which the enumerator failed to count. On the other hand, the large majority of nonwhites who were not counted appeared to live in housing units which were enumerated. Enumerated housing units, however, include what are called "closeout cases," that is, households to which the enumerator was not able to gain admittance after an initial call and two callbacks. In the event of a "closeout case" enumerators were instructed to find out all that they could from neighbors and other persons who might know. Pritzker and Rothwell also pointed out that underenumeration could occur either because enumerators lacked ability or willingness to do a thorough job or because portions of the population were not cooperative. I was myself a staff member of the Population Division of the Bureau for four years during the period of the 1960 Census and can report from my own experience that both of these causes for underenumeration appeared to be present. I observed an obvious reluctance among white female enumerators to make necessary visits in Negro slum areas after dark; and at times I even noted the belief that a full count of poor Negroes was not very important anyway. Furthermore, in observing how census enumerators handled "closeout cases," I saw how difficult it was in Negro slum areas to obtain any cooperation from neighbors. In numerous cases, nextdoor neighbors would deny that they knew anything about the persons who had not been at home during the enumerator's previous visits.

Dr. Conrad Taeuber, Assistant Director for Demographic Fields, U. S. Bureau of the Census, gave the next paper, entitled "Needed Innovations in 1970 Census Data Collection Procedures: A Census View." Taeuber repeated the views of Dr. Eckler, director of the Bureau of the Census, that additional efforts to improve enumeration in areas especially difficult for census taking would require additional funds in the order of magnitude of at least $10 million. Taeuber reported on plans for the Bureau's special pretest in Philadelphia during the fall of 1967 specifically to try out new and more costly procedures for dealing with underenumeration in congested areas. Taeuber also described the list of all housing units in the nation which is to be prepared prior to the 1970 Census and which will be based on commercially prepared mailing lists supplemented by further addresses supplied by Post Office mail carriers. Taeuber was of the opinion that the use of this advance list would improve the coverage of housing units over that achieved in the 1960 Census.

Professor Everett Lee, chairman of the Department of Sociology, University of Massachusetts, Amherst, and chairman of the Committee on

Population Statistics of the Population Association of America, delivered the fourth paper entitled "Needed Improvements in Census Data
Collection Procedures with Special Reference to the Disadvantaged."
Lee pointed out that the population of counties, cities, towns, and
other small areas can change very rapidly, and that even more rapid
changes can occur in the white and nonwhite components of the population. Accordingly, he asserted there was urgent need for a census
to be taken every five years rather than every ten, as at present. A
second important suggestion made by Lee was that the census be taken
in two stages. The initial stage would collect information on certain
basic items but would also serve as a sampling frame for the second
stage in which additional questions would be asked. The proportion to
be sampled in the second stage could be determined on the basis of
characteristics of persons determined from the first stage. Such a
procedure would allow for a larger proportion of small minority groups
to be interviewed in the second stage, and so for the first time we
would be able to obtain data on small groups with sampling reliability
equivalent to that for the larger ones. Such a procedure would produce much better statistics for Negroes, Puerto Ricans, American Indians, and Mexicans.

Dr. Robert Grove, director of the Division of Vital Statistics, National Center for Health Statistics, Public Health Service, delivered the fifth paper "Vital Statistics for the Negro, Puerto Rican,
and Mexican Populations: Present Quality and Plans for Improvement."
Grove stated that nonwhite birth registration was almost 97 percent complete in 1965, compared to 99 percent completeness of registration of

white births.  It was impossible to estimate the completeness of death registration by color, but Grove believed that it was comparable to the completeness of birth registration.  A disturbing aspect of the mortality data for nonwhites, however, was the fact that a matching of death certificates for persons who died shortly after the 1960 Census against the Census schedules revealed a large degree of unreliability in the reporting of age for nonwhites.  For many ten-year age groups the discrepancy was greater than 10 percent.  Unfortunately, however, this match does not allow one to determine separately the degree of inaccuracy in age reporting of either the census or the death certificate.  Grove also reported that vital statistics suffer because race or minority group identification is not always available.  For example, several states do not require the reporting of color on either the marriage or divorce certificate.  Moreover, vital statistics tabulations present data for the two broad groups of white and nonwhite rather than separate data for Negroes, and no national vital statistics data are available either for the Puerto Ricans or for the Mexicans in the United States.  The decennial census makes a special tabulation of persons of Spanish surname in five southwestern states, a group very largely of Mexican origin.  Grove indicated that a similar tabulation could be made for vital records.  However, such a procedure would obviously involve added expense.

The final paper, "Needed Statistics for Minority Groups in Metropolitan Areas," was delivered by Professor Daniel O. Price of the Department of Sociology, University of Texas.  Price made a strong plea for the inclusion in the census of a question on social security numbers. He emphasized that at present the decennial censuses give us only a series of cross-sectional views of the population and that we cannot develop from this series a longitudinal picture of how individuals change over time. For example, we now have no way of measuring how many persons, over time, enter or leave a state of poverty. A question on social security numbers in two or more consecutive censuses would enable us to perform the appropriate matching of census schedules which would provide us with much significant data of this type. Price mentioned other types of data not now gathered that he believed should be obtained from future surveys. Particularly important, in his opinion, would be a measurement of student scholastic achievement. He pointed out that it could then be determined to what extent Negroes suffer employment discrimination in comparison to whites on the same level of scholastic achievement.

It had been decided, in planning the conference, that only those recommendations that were approved by at least two thirds of all the participants were to be made official. The recommendations finally approved and reprinted in this volume thus represent points upon which all or almost all of the participants could agree. Price's recommendation that the social security number be included in the 1970 and subsequent censuses aroused considerable controversy during the conference and was not acceptable to the required proportion of participants. While recognizing the value to social science of such a question, many of the participants felt that it would make possible the linkage of too many diverse records and thus represented an undue invasion of personal privacy. Since the recommendations are not lengthy there is no point in summarizing them here.  However, one idea expressed in them is so important that it deserves repetition.  This is the conclusion that "where a group defined by racial or ethnic terms, and concentrated in specific political jurisdictions, is significantly undercounted in relation to other groups, then individual members of that group are thereby deprived of the constitutional right to equal representation in the House of Representatives and, by inference, in other legislative bodies," and furthermore that "individual members of such a group are thereby deprived of their right to equal protection of the laws as provided by Section I of the 14th Amendment to the Constitution in that they are deprived of their entitlement to partake in federal and other programs designed for areas and populations with their characteristics."

The Conference on Social Statistics and the City received extensive nationwide publicity in newspapers and weekly news magazines. Several leading newspapers, including The Minneapolis Tribune, The New York Times, The Washington Post, and The Washington Star, were prompted to write editorials concerning its findings and recommendations.  Perhaps the strongest statement of support for the aims of the conference came from The Washington Star which declared, ". . . the conference seems to us well justified in asking Congress to appropriate more funds to the Census Bureau, the National Center of Health Statistics, and the Bureau of Labor Statistics to improve census procedures.  The 1960 Census cost around $105 million.  When one considers that multi-billion-dollar aid programs are based on this information, the addition of whatever money is needed to assure reliable data would

surely be a wise investment."


David M. Heer
Harvard School of Public Health

Boston, Massachusetts
December 1967

COMPLETENESS OF COVERAGE OF THE NONWHITE POPULATION IN

THE 1960 CENSUS AND CURRENT ESTIMATES,

AND SOME IMPLICATIONS[*]


Jacob S. Siegel
U. S. Bureau of the Census


## Introduction

It is widely believed that the census counts for Negroes are
quite defective. Some infer this from reading the Census publications, others infer it from working with the data, and still others
assume it on the basis of the presumed difficulties of taking a census in Negro areas. The evidence supports this belief. The magnitude of the errors in the census counts is less well known. They
are a principal subject of concern in this paper. I want to extend
the discussion, however, to consider a number of other topics, particularly the effect of the errors in the counts on current estimates
of population and on various commonly used descriptive and analytic
measures of Negro population.

In view of our relative lack of specific information regarding

[*]The writer wishes to acknowledge the technical assistance of
Richard Irwin of the Bureau of the Census in the preparation of this
paper. He also benefited from the critical reading of the paper by
several other Census Bureau staff members, particularly Morris
Hansen, Leon Pritzker, Naomi D. Rothwell, Henry S. Shryock, Conrad
Taeuber, and Joseph Waksberg.

Negroes, the discussion which follows is based on data for the non-white population. Since Negroes make up the bulk (over 90 percent) of the nonwhite population in the United States, the data for nonwhites may be used to represent the Negro population rather well. Little is specifically known about the quality of Census data for the other principal nonwhite racial group (that is, American Indians) or for Puerto Ricans and Mexican Americans. I have not been able to conduct the research necessary to advance our limited inferential knowledge here. This paper, therefore, will largely concern itself with (1) the extent of the undercoverage of the nonwhite population in total and by age and sex in the 1960 Census, (2) the basis of these findings, (3) some demographic factors affecting the change in coverage between 1950 and 1960 and between 1960 and 1970, (4) the extent of understatement of the Census Bureau's current estimates, including those in the Current Population Survey, and (5) the implications of the findings for some of the demographic characteristics of the nonwhite population.

As the paper by Pritzker and Rothwell indicates, the Census Bureau has been aware of and concerned about deficiencies in its coverage of the population for some time. Furthermore, the Bureau has been rather candid in acknowledging these deficiencies and, when it could measure them satisfactorily, in publishing the results for the benefit of users of Census data. The paper by Pritzker and Rothwell alludes briefly to the historical efforts at evaluation of the census counts and to the alternative ways in which the problem has been studied. The evaluation programs of 1950 and 1960 generally employed case-by-case checking techniques involving reinterviews and matching against independent lists and records, with concomitant studies by the methods

of demographic analysis. The case-by-case checking techniques have

serious limitations as methods of establishing the coverage of the

total population (that is, net underenumeration) and the accuracy of

the data by age, sex, and color (that is, net undercounts representing

the combined effect of net underenumeration and misclassification by

age, sex, or color). For this reason, we turned to use of the results

obtained by the methods of demographic analysis. These methods de-

pend upon the logical consistency of demographic data combined from a

variety of sources, and attempt to employ independent data and tech-

niques, for example, estimates based on birth statistics and "expected

sex ratios" (see below). The analytical approach has its limitations

also, particularly the difficulty of achieving sufficient independence

and the uncertainty as to the completeness of the data on births,

deaths, and immigration.

Our joint research convinces us that the reinterview and record-

check studies of 1960 and 1950 do not provide adequate estimates of

the coverage of the nonwhite population in the 1960 and 1950 Censuses

and that the estimates derived by demographic analysis are more rea-

sonable indications of the extent of error. The present paper, then,

accepts the estimates developed by the "analytic" method for 1960 and

1950 as a point of departure. The basic research, methodology, and

results are summarized in a paper prepared by M. Zelnik and the present

author and presented originally at the 1966 Annual Meeting of the

American Statistical Association.[1] That paper is reproduced in the

---

[1] Jacob S. Siegel and Melvin Zelnik, "An Evaluation of Coverage
in the Census of Population by Techniques of Demographic Analysis and

present volume because it is considered a companion to this one. The

sets of figures on the net undercounts of the 1960 and 1950 Census

population by color, age, and sex, given in the present paper and

adapted from the previous one, do not necessarily represent the true

errors in the census counts but merely the particular sets we have

selected for working purposes.[2]  I want to emphasize that these are

rough estimates of the undercoverage. We do not have any way of mea-

suring these errors precisely. Additional research could be under-

taken which might, possibly, provide improved and additional measures

of coverage. For example, we have not yet fully evaluated the data

on Medicare entitlements as a basis for measuring the accuracy of the

count of aged persons in the 1960 Census. We do not have any esti-

mates of underenumeration for geographic areas within the United States.

We plan to continue our studies as resources permit, and we plan, in

particular, to reexamine the estimates for 1960 and 1950 when the 1970

Census results are available. In the meantime, the present figures

will serve as useful guides.

---

by Composite Methods," <u>Proceedings of the Social Statistics Section,</u>
<u>1966, American Statistical Association</u>, pp. 71-85.  See also in the
same publication the paper by Eli S. Marks and Joseph Waksberg,
"Evaluation of Coverage in the 1960 Census of Population through
Case-by-Case Checking," pp. 62-70.

[2]The figures for nonwhites for 1960 correspond to those labeled
"preferred composite based on demographic analysis" in Table 6, and
"1950 Coale estimates extended to 1960--B" in Table 3 of the Siegel-
Zelnik paper cited previously. The figures for nonwhites for 1950
correspond to those labeled "1950--Coale" in Table 3. The figures
for whites correspond to "1950--Series P-25, No. 310" and "1960--
Series P-25, No. 310--B" in Table 2. The estimates of the percentage net undercount in the present paper differ from those in the
Siegel-Zelnik paper in that the net undercounts are here expressed
as a percentage of the corrected population rather than of the census population.

Completeness of the 1960 Census Counts for Nonwhites

Principal Findings.  I turn now to a consideration of our principal findings relating to coverage of the nonwhite population in the
1960 Census and, to a more limited degree, in the 1950 Census.  By
comparison with coverage for whites, coverage of nonwhites in these
censuses was particularly deficient.  Our studies suggest that the
1960 Census counted about 98 percent of the resident white population
but only about $90\frac{1}{2}$ percent of the resident nonwhite population (Table
1).  In 1950 the general picture was about the same, but a small gain
in coverage between 1950 and 1960 is implied:  in 1950 $97\frac{1}{2}$ percent of
the white population and $88\frac{1}{2}$ percent of the nonwhite population were
enumerated.  Of the estimated total net underenumeration of 5.7 million persons in the 1960 Census, 2.1 million or 38 percent were nonwhite.  The amount of underenumeration was about the same in the 1950
Census:  an estimated total net underenumeration of 5.7 million of
which 2.1 million were nonwhite.

Very substantial improvement was achieved in the enumeration of
nonwhite children between 1950 and 1960 (Table 2).  The undercount
rate for children under the age of 5 dropped from 9.5 percent in 1950
to 7.1 percent in 1960; the rate in 1940 was 15.2 percent.  The rate
for children aged 5-14 dropped from 8.4 percent in 1950 to 5.0 percent
in 1960, and the rate for teenagers aged 15-19 declined from 13.0 percent to 11.3 percent.  Improvement in coverage did not appear to
characterize young adults aged 20-39 years.  In 1960 this group had an
estimated net undercount of about 12.5 percent, whereas in 1950 the
estimate for this group was 10.8 percent.

Our studies indicate a substantially greater underenumeration of males than of females among nonwhites. The figures show an 11 percent underenumeration rate for males and an 8 percent underenumeration rate for females in 1960. Four males were missed for every three females. In 1950 also, the rate of underenumeration for males was substantially higher than for females (13 percent and 10 percent, respectively). The net undercount of young adult males 20-39 years of age was especially high in 1960: about 17 percent, or one out of every six men, in this age range was omitted. The corresponding rate for women was less than half as great: 7.6 percent, or one out of every thirteen women in this range was omitted. There appears to be an irregular decline in the undercount rate of men, and an irregular rise in the undercount rate of women, above age 40. As a result, from the age group 50-54 the rate for women exceeds that of men. The rates are subject to greater and greater error as one goes up the age scale, however, so that little credence can be placed in the level of the estimates for the group aged 65 and over.

An analysis in terms of sex ratios (males per 100 females) is independent of the absolute level of the percentages of net undercount. A comparison of estimated "actual" sex ratios calculated independently of the census with the "enumerated" ratios for 1960 indicates that the "enumerated" ratios are lower than expected at all ages below 50 for nonwhites, especially at ages 20-49 (Table 3). At ages above 55 the "enumerated" ratios are higher than expected. The comparison of sex ratios suggests an overall omission of three men for every 100 women enumerated. These findings indicate that whatever the extent of omission of nonwhite women may be, there is little question that nonwhite men are missed in relatively greater numbers.

There is evidence from the reinterview studies of 1960 of poorer enumeration of housing units in very large cities and in rural areas than in small and moderate-sized cities and in suburbs. No specific evidence from these studies is available by race relating to city-size variations in coverage, whether of housing units or of persons in enumerated housing units; so we cannot definitely say whether the Negroes in the very large cities are more or less completely counted than Negroes in small or moderate-sized cities or rural areas. There is a basis for suggesting that Negroes are counted most poorly in the very large cities because in 1960 the enumeration in urban slums was more difficult and took longer than in other urban segments and in rural areas. The Pritzker-Rothwell paper offers some valuable conjectures regarding the locus of underenumeration.

Methodological Basis of Findings. The estimates of net under-count for the nonwhite population under 25 years of age in 1960 re-present the differences between the census counts and the estimates of population for these ages based on birth, death, and immigration statistics. The births have been adjusted to include an allowance for underregistration derived from two national registration tests conducted in 1940 and 1950. The results of these tests have been in-terpolated and extrapolated to cover every year from 1935 to 1960. (The tests showed that 18 percent of nonwhite births were not reg-istered in 1940 and $6\frac{1}{2}$ percent were not in 1950). On this basis, rates of net undercount were derived for persons under age 5 in 1940, under age 15 in 1950, and under age 25 in 1960. These estimates of net undercount are considered highly reliable since the corrected population figures are largely independent of census data and depend on adjusted birth statistics.

Given the estimates of net undercount for nonwhite children in 1940 and 1950, Coale developed estimates of net undercount at the higher ages by an iterative technique, on the general hypothesis that the age patterns of net undercounts were similar in the 1930, 1940, and 1950 Censuses.[3] More specifically, he assumed that the percentage of net undercount at a given age in the 1930 Census was equal to the lower of the percentages of undercount at the same age in 1940 and 1950. By aging the 1930 corrected population forward to 1940 and 1950, with allowance for deaths and immigration, net undercounts were derived for the older ages in these years. The least reliable results of this method are for the older ages, since errors tend to accumulate as one works up the age scale. The figures for age group 65 and over were accordingly rejected, and the 1950 Post-Enumeration Survey results were substituted. Some adjustments were then made in the estimates of corrected population to assure reasonably acceptable sex ratios at each age. Overall underenumeration for 1950 was obtained by combining the undercounts at each age.

The net undercounts of nonwhite population in 1960 were then derived by carrying the 1950 corrected population forward to 1960

---

[3] Ansley J. Coale, "The Population of the United States in 1950 Classified by Age, Sex, and Color--A Revision of Census Figures," Journal of the American Statistical Association, Vol. 50, No. 1 (March 1955), pp. 16-54.

with appropriate allowances for deaths and immigration.[4] Reasonable
ratios of males to females in the corrected population in 1960 were
assured by substituting estimates of the corrected number of males
obtained by applying expected sex ratios to the corrected number of
females at each age. In most ages this modification had little effect. On the other hand, the change in the age group 65 and over was
particularly large. The expected sex ratios were derived by a technique largely independent of census data that employed various ratios
based on vital statistics. In brief, the sex ratio of births as recorded or estimated for the years since 1885 was projected forward to
each later age and calendar year by the use of a series of current
life table survival rates (from various official life tables combined
as quasi-generation life tables). The results were then adjusted for
the cumulative effects to 1960 of net civilian and military movement
to and from the United States and excess war mortality. While the
expected sex ratios are considered fairly reliable in general, they
are subject to progressively greater error with increases in age.[5]

The estimates of net undercounts for whites under age 25 in 1960
and under age 15 in 1950 were derived by the same method as those for
nonwhites. The estimates for older ages are based on an entirely dif-

---

[4]Melvin Zelnik, "An Examination of Alternative Estimates of Net
Census Undercount, by Age, Sex, and Color: 1950 and 1960," paper contributed to the annual meeting of the Population Association of America, New York, April 1966. See also the summary of the paper in Population Index (July 1966).

[5]Jacob S. Siegel, Summary of "Estimates of the True Sex Ratios
of the United States Population by Age and Color, in 1960," Population Index (July 1966).

ferent method, involving the reconstruction of annual births from data from several censuses and the aging of these forward to 1950.[6] Given the corrected population in 1950, the estimates for 1960 were derived in the same manner as for nonwhites.

Some Demographic Factors Affecting Change in Coverage. In considering the relative effectiveness of the enumeration of nonwhites in 1960 and 1950 and the prospects for improvement of coverage in 1970, it seems useful to take note of some of the population changes in these periods that may have affected or that will affect the enumeration situation, particularly changes in geographic distribution, changes in age composition, and changes in household characteristics. I have not attempted a thorough analysis along these lines but should merely like to offer some suggestive observations here.

The data show a greater concentration of Negroes in large cities in 1960 than in 1950. The proportion of the Negro population living in cities of one-half million or more rose from 24 percent in 1950 to 30 percent in 1960. Moreover, the Negro population has apparently been growing rapidly in the expanding deteriorated parts of these cities, and it is precisely in such areas that we believe enumeration is least complete. We should, therefore, expect a substantial reduction in coverage as a result of increasing urbanization. Yet, theoretical computations, based on the actual change in the proportions living in large cities between 1950 and 1960 and on an ex-

---

[6] A. J. Coale and M. Zelnik, New Estimates of Fertility and Population in the United States (Princeton, N.J.: Princeton University Press, 1963).

treme assumption regarding the relative magnitude of the rate of underenumeration of nonwhites in the large cities and the rate of underenumeration in other areas in 1950, indicate only a negligible increase in the overall rate of underenumeration.  If, for example, the
rate of underenumeration in cities of 500,000 or more is assumed to
be twice as great as elsewhere, the overall rate would increase by
only 0.5 percent, from 11.5 percent to 12.0 percent, between 1950 and
1960.  Inasmuch as the estimated actual rate of underenumeration of
nonwhites in 1960 was 9.5 percent, substantial "real" overall improvement occurred in spite of the increased population concentration in
large cities.  This concentration has apparently been continuing during the current decade.  Again, contrary to expectation, this factor
per se is not likely to have any appreciable effect on the national
level of underenumeration of the nonwhite population in 1970.

In view of the considerable variation in undercount rates by
age and sex, it seemed useful to examine the effect of shifts in the
age and sex composition of the nonwhite population between 1950 and
1960 on the overall level of coverage of nonwhites.  It appears, however, that the shifts in age and sex composition tended to have little effect.  Given the rates of net undercount for nonwhite males and
females at each age in 1950, corresponding to an overall net underenumeration of 11.5 percent in 1950, we would expect an overall net
underenumeration of 11.2 percent in 1960, whereas the estimated actual
rate was 9.5 percent.  These figures suggest that most of the reduction in the rate of underenumeration of nonwhites between 1950 and
1960 was "real" improvement and that only a small part can be ac-

counted for by a change in the age-sex composition.

Changes in the age-sex composition of the nonwhite population in the current decade will also tend to have little effect on the overall rate of nonwhite underenumeration expected in 1970 on the basis of the 1960 Census undercounts for each age-sex group. If the rates of net undercount in 1960 at each age for nonwhites are applied to the popu-lation by age and sex expected in 1970, the resulting theoretical over-all rate of nonwhite underenumeration would be the same as estimated for 1960, that is, 9.5 percent. However, due to the increase in popu-lation between 1960 and 1970, the amount of nonwhite underenumeration implied by these calculations would be 2.6 million, as compared with 2.1 million in 1960, and nonwhite underenumeration would make up nearly 40 percent of the total theoretical underenumeration of 6.8 million. If underenumeration of nonwhites is kept to the same abso-lute level as in 1960 and 1950, that is, 2.1 million, a substantial reduction in the rate to 7.8 percent would be implied.

Finally, among the possibly important demographic factors af-fecting change in coverage of nonwhites between 1950 and 1960, I would mention the apparent decline in the proportion of persons not living in households, the decline in the proportion of nonfamily members in households, and the stability in average household size. One could profitably examine these factors further.

## Completeness of Current Population Estimates

*Total Population and Population by Age and Sex.* Let us con-sider next the completeness of the current estimates of total population and population by age and sex shown in the Census Bureau's <u>Current Population Reports</u>, Series P-25 and Series P-20 (also P-60). The various estimates of the total nonwhite and Negro population in Series P-25 for current dates reflect essentially the same <u>absolute</u> level of error as the census counts, inasmuch as the current estimates are derived simply by combining births, deaths, and immigration since the census with the census counts. (This is based on the fact that population change since the last census is measured exactly or quite closely with the data available.) The <u>percentage</u> understatement in postcensal years would, however, be increasingly smaller with the passage of years because of the growth of population since 1960. The net understatement of the total nonwhite population was 8.2 percent in April 1967, as compared with 9.5 percent in April 1960 (Table 1). Between April 1960 and April 1967, the rate of net understatement of whites fell from 2.2 percent to 2.0 percent; hence, the difference between the white and nonwhite rates is narrowing. Given highly accurate estimates of postcensal population change, we have the curious result that the net understatement in our current estimates of total population declines with the lengthening of the postcensal period.

The same amounts and percentages of understatement apply essentially to the estimates of total nonwhite or Negro population in the Series P-20 reports which accompany the tabulations based on the Current Population Survey (CPS), the Census Bureau's national sample survey. These figures variously exclude part of the military population and/or the institutional population, but they agree with the estimates of the total nonwhite population and closely approximate the estimates of the Negro population, in Series P-25, when the same type of population is represented. This is because the CPS estimation procedure involves the use of the "independent" estimates of the population as part of the preparation of the CPS figures.

The net understatement of the postcensal estimates by age in Series P-25 differs from the net undercounts of the 1960 Census by age in an important way. The census undercounts at each age apply approximately to successively older populations with each passing year, so that, for example, in 1965, the 1960 net undercount for ages 10-14 characterizes ages 15-19 and the 1960 net undercount for ages 15-19 characterizes ages 20-24. We may call this shift in age reference the "cohort effect." In most ages, that is, ages 40-44 and over, the cohorts tend with time to diminish in size as a result of the excess of death over immigration, and therefore the percentage net understatement is somewhat larger in 1965 than in 1960 for a given cohort. The opposite is true in the younger ages, where the cohorts increase in size with time as a result of the excess of immigration over deaths. The estimates for the age group under 5 in 1965 have a zero net understatement since they are based on corrected births, recorded deaths, and immigration data. Estimates of the amounts and percentages of net understatement in the Census Bureau's estimates of the nonwhite population by age and sex for July 1965, in comparison with the corresponding figures for whites, are shown in Table 2.

As has been indicated in various technical reports of the Census Bureau, all the estimates based on the Current Population Survey receive a final adjustment to the "independent" national population

estimates by age, sex, and color, which we have been discussing.[7]
This means that the CPS figures for the population of each age, sex,
and color group, as published in Series P-20, have approximately the
same degree of completeness as the estimates for these categories
published in Series P-25.

Current Population Survey Estimates.  The quality of the CPS
data for nonwhites with respect to various social and economic characteristics may be of a different order of magnitude, however.  These
statistics are affected directly both by the fact that the independent
postcensal estimates understate the actual population by age, sex, and
color and by the fact that the "uncontrolled" CPS estimates (that is,
the CPS figures prior to adjustment to the independent estimates by
age, sex, and color) for these categories usually fall below the independent estimates.  The CPS estimation procedure of tying the CPS
figures to independent estimates by age, sex, and color implicitly
assumes that the persons missed by CPS (but covered by the independent
estimates) have the same average characteristics as the persons enumerated.  If the assumption is true, the adjustment of the CPS figures
properly allows for the effect of the deficit in CPS relative to the
independent estimates on the statistics for social and economic characteristics.  The very fact of omission, however, leads one to be-

-----

[7]U. S. Bureau of the Census, The Current Population Survey--A
Report on Methodology, Technical Paper No. 7, U. S. Government Printing Office, Washington, D. C. (1963), Part VII, pp. 53-55; and "Con-
cepts and Methods Used in Manpower Statistics from the Current Population Survey," Current Population Reports, Series P-23, No. 22 (June
1967), pp. 13-14 (also BLS Report, No. 313, of the U. S. Bureau of
Labor Statistics).

lieve that the persons omitted have different characteristics.[8]

Let us consider the magnitude of the deficit in the unadjusted CPS figures in relation to the independent estimates. The overall deficit for the (civilian noninstitutional) nonwhite population has generally been falling for a number of years (Table 4). The discrepancy has been small for females (varying from a deficit in CPS of 1.7 percent in 1962 to an excess in CPS of 1.4 percent in 1966), but substantial for males (varying from a deficit of 6.7 percent in 1962 to a deficit of 3.2 percent in 1966). As judged by the independent estimates, CPS now covers white females less completely than nonwhite females, but in the earlier years of this decade the reverse was true. Coverage of white males and nonwhite males has been about the same for the last three years, but in the earlier years of the decade undercoverage of nonwhite males far exceeded that of white males. The figures thus indicate that CPS coverage of nonwhites is improving, and that CPS coverage of whites is deteriorating, relative to the independent estimates.

The average differences by age between the unadjusted CPS estimates and the independent estimates have been summarized for the period April 1962 to December 1966 (Table 5). (The survey data have been ad-

---

[8]The estimates for social and economic characteristics from the survey are also subject to various other types of errors in addition to those arising because persons enumerated in CPS may be a biased sample of all persons in terms of these characteristics. The estimates are subject to sampling error, errors in the field (nonresponse and misclassification), and errors in compilation. Nonresponse (principally noninterview of about 4 percent of the households) represents a possible source of bias, although an adjustment is made to account for noninterviews or for incomplete interviews. There is also a small net error arising from the processing operations.

justed to independent estimates based on the 1960 Census since April
1962.)  Before the adjustment to the independent estimates, the CPS
figures for nonwhite males had a deficit of 5 percent in the total
fourteen years and over, and deficits exceeding 4 percent in each
"control" age group from 18 through 49.  The largest deficit was 19
percent for the age group 20-24.  Considerable excess in CPS was
registered at ages 65-69 (13 percent).  Deficits of the order of 3 to
7 percent appear for nonwhite females in the age range 18-39, and a
tremendous excess (23 percent) is indicated for the group aged 65-69.
Apparently, not only do both the census and CPS suffer from a substantial degree of undercoverage, but the CPS is generally more deficient than the census, especially with respect to coverage of nonwhite males aged 20-24.

The indicated understatement of CPS with respect to the independent estimates and the indicated undercount in the census may be
taken in combination and manipulated to determine (a) the total percentage understatement of the unadjusted CPS figures in relation to
the corrected population, (b) the part of the total understatement
which is contributed by deficits of the unadjusted CPS figures with
respect to the current estimates, and (c) the part which is contributed by deficits in the current estimates.  Estimates of the total
understatement in CPS have been worked out for the population aged 14
and over by color and sex, for each year 1960 through 1965 (Table 6),
and for the population aged 14 and over, by age, sex, and color, for
1965 (Table 7).  For this purpose, first, estimates of corrected
population by age and sex for 1965 were calculated, using the 1960

Census net undercounts, and were compared with the estimates of population shown in Series P-25 for 1965. The differences represent the percentage understatements in the current estimates of population (Table 2). The total understatement in CPS in 1965 was derived by combining (that is, multiplying) (a) the CPS deficits in relation to the current estimates in 1965 with (b) the deficits in the current estimates in relation to the corrected population in 1965. (The combination of the 1960 Census percentage undercounts for a given age group in Table 2 and the percentage undercounts in CPS in Table 5 does not correctly measure the total error, principally because the current estimates have approximately the net undercount of the age cohort in 1960 and not the net undercount of the same age group in 1960.)

Our results show that in 1965 the CPS missed more than 10 percent of the corrected nonwhite male population in all (eleven) age groups 14 and over, except ages 14-19 and 65 and over, and more than 5 percent in every age group 14 and over. The CPS missed more than 10 percent of the nonwhite female population in four out of eleven age groups and more than 5 percent in all but two of the groups. The largest omission occurred at ages 20-24 for nonwhite males (30 percent), of whom 12 percent were omitted by both the independent estimate and CPS and 18 percent by the CPS alone. Over the whole age range 20-39, the CPS missed 25 percent of the nonwhite male population, to which the independent estimate contributed 17 percent and the CPS added another 8 percent. In general, the contribution of the CPS alone to the total understatement was much smaller than the contribution of the independent estimate. This was especially true for non-

white females, since the CPS exceeded the independent estimates in
several age groups. The deficit of the CPS alone was very large only
for males and females aged 20-24 and males aged 60-64. Over all ages
14 and over, the CPS missed 17 percent of the males, of whom only 4
percent were "taken care of" by adjustment to the independent estimates; 9 percent of the females were missed by CPS and virtually none
of them were "taken care of" by the adjustment.

In view of the omission of one out of four nonwhite males aged
20-39 in CPS in 1965 and in view of the considerable effort and care
that have gone into the design and conduct of the CPS, it is clearly
extremely difficult to achieve even a fair level of coverage of this
group in particular, and of nonwhites in general, in even a very carefully designed and executed sample survey.

The implications of such considerable undercount rates for nonwhite males in the CPS for the quality of the CPS data on socioeconomic characteristics, such as labor force, employment, unemployment, and the corresponding rates, are not clear. We must be quite
wary about assuming that all figures based on the CPS are low. The
adjustment to independent population estimates for each age, sex, and
color group eliminates a part--generally the smaller part, as we have
seen--of the undercoverage in the age-sex totals, but the absolute
figures in all or nearly all categories remain low. The more important question concerns the accuracy of the estimate of the proportion in the labor force, the proportion of the labor force which
is employed or unemployed, and other such proportions or rates. The
application of the same adjustment factor, for undercoverage of the

CPS vis-à-vis the independent estimates, to the CPS data on specific

social and economic characteristics in a given age-sex-color group

does not change the proportions in the age-sex-color group having

these characteristics. If the specific socioeconomic status cate-

gories in the age-sex-color group are equally well represented by

CPS in relation to the actual numbers in these categories, the CPS

proportions or rates will reflect the true proportion or rates. For

some characteristics, however, it is quite possible that persons in

a given category (for example, employed) may be much more completely

reported than persons in the "complementary" category or categories

(for example, unemployed). Under these circumstances, the first

category is overstated, and the number in the complementary cate-

gory or categories is understated, relative to their total; that is,

the first proportion is too high and the second is too low. For

example, if the Negro males at a given age who are missed in the CPS

have a higher unemployment rate than the Negro males of this age who

are enumerated, both the number of unemployed at this age and the un-

employment rate are understated by the CPS. If, on the other hand,

those missed have a lower unemployment rate, this rate is overstated

by the CPS.

Let us consider an example using some extreme assumptions. If

we assume that, in a given age-sex group, 25 percent of the popula-

tion and the labor force is missed by the CPS and that the unemploy-

ment rate for those missed is twice as high as that for the enumerated

labor force, then the corrected unemployment rate would be 25 percent

greater than reported; for example, if the reported unemployment rate is 8 percent, the corrected rate would be 10 percent. It is clear that it takes a very high undercount rate and a disproportionately high unemployment rate for the missed persons to produce a gross misrepresentation of the unemployment rate in the reported statistics. I want to emphasize that we do not really know about the relative unemployment rate of missed persons and enumerated persons. It is possible that persons missed tend to have a higher-than-average employment rate; they may be missed because they are more often away from home at work when the enumerator calls.

We may consider another example, the proportion of Negro families headed by females. The CPS tells us that in 1965 one quarter of all Negro families were headed by females. Whether the CPS proportion is too low or too high depends on the sex composition, family status, and relationship of persons omitted by CPS. We are reasonably sure that a larger proportion of males than of females are omitted in CPS. One may hazard the guess, on the basis of the 1960 Census reinterview studies, that a higher proportion of persons omitted than of persons included in the survey are nonfamily members. Whether male heads constitute a disproportionate part of the family members omitted is not known, but this is quite possible. For most male heads who were omitted and could have been enumerated, a female head would be displaced, so that the effect on the proportion of families headed by females is magnified. Thus, it is quite possible that among Negroes the proportion of families headed by females is overstated in the official figures. Trial calculations suggest, however, that the omissions from the CPS can account for only a small part of the gap between the proportion of Negro families headed by females and the proportion of white families headed by females (9 percent in 1965). (The proportion of Negro families headed by females may be understated in the official figures if female heads constitute a disproportionate part of family members omitted, but the understatement would necessarily be very small or negligible.)

## Further Demographic Implications of the Findings

Effect on Growth Rate and Age-Sex Composition. It is to be expected that the census will miss some people. We should become concerned about the omissions only when either the absolute numbers omitted or the rates of omission become sizable, when substantial variations occur between geographic areas or significant segments of the population, or when important analytic measures are seriously affected by the omissions. For a consideration of the last point, we turn next to a comparison of some of the characteristics of the population shown by corrected population counts and estimates with those shown by the counts and estimates as published.

As would be expected, the actual percentage of nonwhites in the total population is a little higher than indicated in the published reports. The estimated "actual" figure was 12.2 percent instead of 11.4 percent in April 1960, and 12.8 percent instead of 12.0 percent in April 1967 (Table 8). Although the level of the corrected figures would be a little higher, the trend in the proportion of nonwhites from 1950 to 1967 would be about the same whether the figures are corrected or not.

The overall growth rate of the nonwhite population between April 1960 and April 1967 would be reduced to a small extent by substitution of corrected numbers, from 16.4 percent to 14.9 percent. The corresponding figures for whites would hardly change.

In view of the fact that census net undercounts vary sharply by age, the "cohort effect" tends to distort various measures for postcensal years involving age data, such as postcensal growth rates by age, the percentage age distribution, the median age, the dependency ratio. When the figures are adjusted for net undercounts, the "cohort effect" is eliminated.

To measure the modification of postcensal changes by age resulting from the use of corrected population estimates, corrected estimates of postcensal change for July 1, 1960 to 1965, and April 1, 1950 to 1960, have been compared with the original estimates (Table 9). Rather pronounced modifications appear in the postcensal population changes for particular age groups for the nonwhite population. Several age groups appear to have grown much less rapidly than indicated by the uncorrected figures, and several appear to have grown much more rapidly. On the basis of the corrected figures, the original percentage increase for young children between 1960 and 1965 is sharply reduced. Whereas the uncorrected figures indicate a 10 percent increase for the nonwhite population under age 5, the corrected figures show an increase of only 2 percent. (This large modification results from the fact that the so-called "uncorrected" figure for the group under age 5 in 1965 is really a corrected estimate based on births adjusted for underregistration, so that only the population estimates for 1960 are actually changed in the new calculations.) The changes for ages 15-24 and 45-54 between 1960 and 1965 were reduced appreciably by use of corrected figures, whereas the changes at ages 55-64 and 65 and over were increased appreciably. Different age cohorts are being compared in the ten-year changes from 1950 to 1960 for a given age group from those being compared in the five-year changes from 1960 to 1965 for that age group, so that the direction and magnitude of the modifications are often quite different for the two periods. Because net undercounts are smaller and less variable from age to age for whites than for nonwhites, modifications in the original percentage changes for whites are much smaller; hence, the official published figures for whites reflect the actual changes more faithfully.

In spite of the fact that the census net undercounts for non-whites are quite variable from age to age, the percentage distribution by age of the nonwhite population based on the original figures in 1950 and 1960 gives a satisfactory indication of the corrected distribution by age and of the variation from the age distribution for whites. This is true also for 1965, in spite of the distortion added in 1965 by the "cohort effect" previously referred to. Furthermore, the pattern of changes in the age distribution between 1960 and 1965 and between 1950 and 1960 is not seriously distorted by the uncorrected figures.

These relations are reflected in "indices of dissimilarity" (calculated by taking one half of the sum of the differences in the percentages at each age without regard to sign), which measure the degree of dissimilarity between the various percentage distributions expressed in terms of broad age groups (Table 10). The index of dissimilarity comparing the uncorrected and corrected nonwhite age distributions in 1960 is only 1.6, as contrasted with the index comparing the uncorrected white and nonwhite distributions (8.8) and the index comparing the corrected white and nonwhite distributions (8.2) in the same year. That is, the dissimilarity between the two nonwhite distributions (before and after adjustment) is still small compared with the dissimilarity between the white and nonwhite distributions, whether corrected or not. The same type of analysis using data for 1965 and 1950 gives the same picture. Moreover, the change in the indices resulting from the use of corrected populations to compare distributions at different dates (that is, 1960 and 1965, and 1950 and 1960) is small compared to the size of the indices.

The effect of the corrections on the age distribution of the nonwhite population is summarized in the modifications of the median age resulting from the corrections (Table 11). The median age of the nonwhite population would have been 24.4 years in 1960 instead of 23.5 years if the census counts had conformed to the corrected figures; in 1965 the upward revision would have been even greater, from 21.6 years to 23.1 years. The median age of the white population, which is much higher than that for nonwhites, is hardly affected by the substitution of corrected population figures. The effect of the corrections is to reduce somewhat the gap between the medians of the white and nonwhite populations, for example, from 7.3 years to 5.9 years in 1965. The corrections do not essentially change the picture that the nonwhite population is considerably younger than the white population and that the median age of the nonwhite population has fallen substantially since 1950--and more rapidly than that of the white population in this period.

A substantial reduction in the so-called "dependency ratio" of the nonwhite population occurs when corrected data are substituted for the original figures (Table 12). On this basis the ratio of children under age 18 and of persons aged 65 and over to persons aged 18-64 would be 89 rather than 101 in 1960. For 1965 the corresponding figures are 94 and 102. In view of the fact that the dependency ratios for whites in these years are little affected by the adjustment, there is a considerable narrowing of the white-nonwhite difference. At the same time, the pattern remains of a much higher dependency rate for nonwhites than for whites. Whether uncorrected or corrected figures are examined, there was a sharp increase in the nonwhite dependency ratio between 1950 and 1960, only a small or moderate rise between 1960 and 1965, and a widening of the white-nonwhite gap since 1950.

We have already stated that a characteristic feature of the enumeration of nonwhites is the relatively greater omission of males than of females, especially at the young adult ages. The sex ratios implied by the corrected population figures for 1960 conform to the sex ratios employed in deriving them. They suggest that the proportions of males are really higher for the total nonwhite population, and at many ages, than shown by the 1960 Census counts, especially at ages 15-24, 25-34, and 35-44. Overall, the sex ratios in 1960 would be expected to be 97.7 rather than 94.7 for the resident population and 98.0 rather than 95.1 for the total population, including Armed Forces overseas (Tables 3 and 13). Although the census counts show

86 males per 100 females at ages 25-34, the corrected figures imply

99 males per 100 females, or 13 more males for every 100 females. At

ages 55-64 and 65 and over the "actual" proportions of males are

lower than implied by the census counts; for example, there should be

only 8 men for every 10 women rather than 9 men for every 10 women at

ages 65 and over. By 1965, because of the "cohort" effect, serious

understatement of the sex ratio has shifted up to ages 25-54 and seri-

ous overstatement to ages 65 and over. Although the white-nonwhite

differences in sex ratios for the total population and at each age are

generally much smaller in the corrected figures than in the uncor-

rected ones, the general pattern of differences remains.

Effect on Vital Rates. The effect of undercoverage in the cen-

sus has been further examined in terms of the effect on vital rates of

various kinds.[9] The birth rate, death rate, natural increase rate,

and total fertility rate (that is, the sum of age-specific birth rates)

of nonwhites in 1960 and 1965 would be reduced by about 8 to 10 percent

by a correction for undercoverage of the population (Table 14). The

corrected figures still indicate a substantial excess of nonwhite fer-

tility over white fertility, a sharp drop in nonwhite fertility be-

tween 1960 and 1965, and a considerable excess of the rate of natural

increase of nonwhites over that of whites. One striking effect of the

correction of death rates is to reverse the white-nonwhite difference,

---

[9]A more detailed examination of the effect of using corrected
data in the calculation of various vital rates and reproduction rates
is given in the paper by Reynolds Farley, "The Quality of Demographic
Data for Non-Whites," presented at the 1967 annual meeting of the
Population Association of America in Cincinnati, Ohio. See also the
paper by Robert D. Grove in this volume.

so that, assuming no underregistration of deaths, the death rate of the nonwhite population would be lower than that of whites. This is accounted for largely by the younger age distribution of nonwhites. If corrected population data are employed, life expectancy of nonwhites at birth in 1959-1961 would be increased by about $1\frac{1}{2}$ years and most of the large white-nonwhite difference would remain.

## Conclusion

The 1960 Census failed to count a substantial portion of the nonwhite population in the United States. It is clear that a disproportionate share of the omissions consisted of young adult males, and it is probable that a disproportionate share occurred in large cities. A highly conjectural inference may be made that the enumeration of Puerto Ricans and other population groups concentrated in the deteriorated sections of our large cities was also rather defective. The failure of the Census to count the population more completely has a pervasive effect on the statistical programs of government and industry. Current estimates and many types of derived data and measures are affected. It has been shown that in many respects the counts and estimates of national population by age, sex, and color do not seriously distort the picture of the demographic situation in the United States as a whole. It is quite probable, however, that serious distortion does occur in the figures for many smaller geographic units within the country, particularly units in cities (such as census tracts, congressional districts, and enumeration districts) where Negroes, Puerto Ricans, and other relatively poor minority groups are concentrated.

Table 1.  ESTIMATED NET UNDERSTATEMENT AND CORRECTED POPULATION, BY
COLOR AND SEX:  APRIL 1, 1967, 1960, AND 1950

(Numbers in thousands.  Figures for 1967 include Armed Forces
overseas; figures for 1960 and 1950 relate to the total resident population. Base of percentages is corrected population.)

| Color, Sex, and Year | Current Estimates or Census Counts | Corrected Population | Net Understatement | |
|---|---|---|---|---|
| | | | Amount | Percent. |
| 1967 | | | | |
| All classes | 198,467 | 204,169 | 5,702 | 2.8 |
| Nonwhite, total | 23,913 | 26,055 | 2,142 | 8.2 |
| Male | 11,618 | 12,834 | 1,216 | 9.5 |
| Female | 12,295 | 13,221 | 926 | 7.0 |
| White, total | 174,554 | 178,114 | 3,560 | 2.0 |
| Male | 86,016 | 88,289 | 2,273 | 2.6 |
| Female | 88,538 | 89,825 | 1,287 | 1.4 |
| 1960 | | | | |
| All classes | 179,323 | 185,025 | 5,702 | 3.1 |
| Nonwhite, total | 20,491 | 22,633 | 2,142 | 9.5 |
| Male | 9,964 | 11,180 | 1,216 | 10.9[1] |
| Female | 10,527 | 11,453 | 926 | 8.1 |
| White, total | 158,832 | 162,392 | 3,560 | 2.2 |
| Male | 78,367 | 80,640 | 2,273 | 2.8 |
| Female | 80,465 | 81,752 | 1,287 | 1.6 |
| 1950[2] | | | | |
| All classes | 151,327 | 157,001 | 5,675 | 3.6 |
| Nonwhite, total | 16,177 | 18,274 | 2,097 | 11.5 |
| Male | 7,932 | 9,122 | 1,190 | 13.0[1] |
| Female | 8,245 | 9,152 | 907 | 9.9 |
| White, total | 135,150 | 138,728 | 3,578 | 2.6 |
| Male | 67,255 | 69,407 | 2,152 | 3.1 |
| Female | 67,895 | 69,321 | 1,426 | 2.1 |

[1]The figures for 1960 and 1950 based on the total population including Armed Forces overseas are 10.8 and 12.8 percent, respectively.

[2]Figures relate to fifty States.

Table 2.  ESTIMATED AMOUNT AND PERCENTAGE OF NET UNDERSTATEMENT OF THE
POPULATION, BY AGE, SEX, AND COLOR, IN THE 1950 AND 1960
CENSUS COUNTS AND THE 1965 CURRENT ESTIMATES

(Numbers in thousands.  Figures for 1965 relate to the total population including Armed Forces overseas.  Figures for 1960 and 1950 relate to the total resident population.  Base of percentages is the
corrected population.  A minus sign (−) denotes an overstatement in
the census count or current estimate.)

| Sex, Color, and Age | 1965 (July 1) Amount | % | 1960 (April 1) Amount | % | 1950 (April 1)[1] Amount | % |
|---|---|---|---|---|---|---|
| NONWHITE | | | | | | |
| Male, all ages | 1,234[2] | 9.9[2] | 1,218[3] | 10.9[3] | 1,165[4] | 12.8[4] |
| 0-4 | -- | -- | 124 | 7.7 | 112 | 9.9 |
| 5-9 | 121 | 7.5 | 78 | 5.7 | 99 | 10.7 |
| 10-14 | 80 | 5.7 | 59 | 5.2 | 52 | 6.6 |
| 15-19 | 60 | 5.3 | 114 | 12.5 | 116 | 15.2 |
| 20-24 | 111 | 12.1 | 133 | 17.5 | 118 | 15.9 |
| 25-29 | 135 | 17.4 | 150 | 19.7 | 128 | 16.6 |
| 30-34 | 155 | 20.1 | 138 | 18.0 | 112 | 16.6 |
| 35-39 | 141 | 18.5 | 107 | 14.5 | 70 | 10.8 |
| 40-44 | 106 | 14.6 | 82 | 12.8 | 102 | 16.6 |
| 45-49 | 82 | 13.2 | 69 | 11.5 | 60 | 11.6 |
| 50-54 | 73 | 12.9 | 97 | 17.8 | 42 | 9.9 |
| 55-59 | 100 | 19.8 | 25 | 5.9 | 48 | 14.4 |
| 60-64 | 25 | 6.8 | 31 | 9.7 | 52 | 19.5 |
| 65 and over | 44 | 6.4 | 11 | 1.8 | 54 | 10.8 |
| Female, all ages | 933[2] | 7.3[2] | 924[3] | 8.1[3] | 893[4] | 9.8[4] |
| 0-4 | -- | -- | 101 | 6.4 | 101 | 9.1 |
| 5-9 | 97 | 6.1 | 66 | 4.8 | 83 | 9.1 |
| 10-14 | 68 | 4.9 | 47 | 4.2 | 51 | 6.5 |
| 15-19 | 49 | 4.3 | 91 | 10.1 | 82 | 10.8 |
| 20-24 | 89 | 9.7 | 75 | 9.6 | 58 | 7.5 |
| 25-29 | 78 | 9.8 | 67 | 8.7 | 57 | 7.4 |
| 30-34 | 70 | 9.1 | 46 | 5.9 | 57 | 8.3 |
| 35-39 | 48 | 6.2 | 47 | 6.2 | 19 | 2.9 |
| 40-44 | 47 | 6.3 | 42 | 6.4 | 95 | 15.3 |
| 45-49 | 42 | 6.5 | 52 | 8.4 | 56 | 10.8 |
| 50-54 | 52 | 8.8 | 103 | 18.2 | 59 | 13.7 |
| 55-59 | 104 | 19.4 | 45 | 10.0 | 79 | 23.0 |
| 60-64 | 44 | 10.8 | 50 | 14.1 | 73 | 26.5 |
| 65 and over | 145 | 16.0 | 92 | 12.2 | 23 | 4.7 |

(continued.)

Table 2 (continued).

| Sex, Color, and Age | 1965 (July 1) Amount | % | 1960 (April 1) Amount | % | 1950 (April 1)[1] Amount | % |
|---|---|---|---|---|---|---|
| WHITE | | | | | | |
| Male, all ages | 2,268[2] | 2.6[2] | 2,256[3] | 2.8[3] | 2,168[4] | 3.1[4] |
| 0-4 | -- | -- | 117 | 2.0 | 327 | 4.3 |
| 5-9 | 168 | 1.8 | 205 | 2.4 | 184 | 3.0 |
| 10-14 | 206 | 2.4 | 194 | 2.5 | 49 | 1.0 |
| 15-19 | 203 | 2.6 | 233 | 3.8 | 197 | 4.0 |
| 20-24 | 222 | 3.5 | 209 | 4.3 | 296 | 5.6 |
| 25-29 | 201 | 3.9 | 208 | 4.2 | 279 | 4.9 |
| 30-34 | 202 | 4.0 | 167 | 3.1 | 229 | 4.3 |
| 35-39 | 190 | 3.5 | 142 | 2.5 | 104 | 2.1 |
| 40-44 | 132 | 2.4 | 97 | 1.9 | 156 | 3.3 |
| 45-49 | 103 | 2.0 | 77 | 1.6 | 90 | 2.2 |
| 50-54 | 83 | 1.8 | 159 | 3.6 | 83 | 2.2 |
| 55-59 | 159 | 3.8 | 15 | 0.4 | 178 | 5.0 |
| 60-64 | 19 | 0.6 | 97 | 3.0 | 102 | 3.5 |
| 65 and over | 381 | 5.0 | 276 | 3.8 | -107 | -2.0 |
| Female, all ages | 1,319[2] | 1.5[2] | 1,297[3] | 1.6[3] | 1,428[4] | 2.1[4] |
| 0-4 | -- | -- | 102 | 1.2 | 264 | 3.7 |
| 5-9 | 94 | 1.1 | 126 | 1.6 | 142 | 2.4 |
| 10-14 | 127 | 1.6 | 108 | 1.5 | 52 | 1.1 |
| 15-19 | 123 | 1.7 | 144 | 2.4 | 84 | 1.8 |
| 20-24 | 134 | 2.2 | 121 | 2.4 | 83 | 1.6 |
| 25-29 | 126 | 2.5 | 68 | 1.4 | 17 | 0.3 |
| 30-34 | 67 | 1.4 | 32 | 0.6 | 5 | 0.1 |
| 35-39 | 48 | 0.9 | -11 | -0.2 | -72 | -1.4 |
| 40-44 | -17 | -0.3 | -11 | -0.2 | 92 | 2.0 |
| 45-49 | -5 | -0.1 | 35 | 0.7 | 61 | 1.5 |
| 50-54 | 30 | 0.6 | 194 | 4.2 | 102 | 2.6 |
| 55-59 | 190 | 4.3 | 62 | 1.6 | 254 | 7.1 |
| 60-64 | 67 | 1.8 | 151 | 4.2 | 206 | 6.8 |
| 65 and over | 333 | 3.5 | 176 | 2.1 | 138 | 2.2 |

- Number or percent is zero.

[1] Figures relate to fifty States.

[2] Total amounts were obtained by summing estimates at each age and differ somewhat from required totals as shown for 1960 and 1967 in Table 1. Required percentages are 9.7 for nonwhite males and 7.2 for nonwhite females. The required percentages for white males and females are the same as shown.

[3] Figures differ somewhat from required totals as shown for 1960 in Table 1.

[4] Figures differ somewhat from required totals as shown for 1950 in Table 1.

Table 3. DEFICIT OF "ENUMERATED" SEX RATIOS IN COMPARISON WITH ESTIMATED "ACTUAL" SEX RATIOS, BY COLOR AND AGE: 1960

(Males per 100 females. Figures relate to the total resident population. A minus sign (-) denotes an excess in the "enumerated" sex ratio.)

| Age | Nonwhite | | | White | | |
|---|---|---|---|---|---|---|
| | Enumerated | Estimated Actual | Difference | Enumerated | Estimated Actual | Difference |
| Total, all ages | 94.7 | 97.6 | 2.9 | 97.4 | 98.6 | 1.2 |
| Under 5 | 99.9 | 101.4 | 1.5 | 104.0 | 104.8 | 0.8 |
| 5-9 | 100.0 | 100.7 | 0.7 | 104.0 | 104.9 | 0.9 |
| 10-14 | 100.1 | 101.1 | 1.0 | 103.8 | 104.8 | 1.0 |
| 15-19 | 97.8 | 99.5 | 1.7 | 101.1 | 102.9 | 1.8 |
| 20-24 | 89.1 | 97.5 | 8.4 | 96.3 | 98.5 | 2.2 |
| 25-29 | 87.0 | 98.9 | 11.9 | 97.7 | 100.5 | 2.8 |
| 30-34 | 85.8 | 98.4 | 12.6 | 97.2 | 99.6 | 2.4 |
| 35-39 | 89.4 | 98.0 | 8.6 | 95.7 | 98.4 | 2.7 |
| 40-44 | 90.4 | 97.0 | 6.6 | 96.4 | 98.5 | 2.1 |
| 45-49 | 93.8 | 97.2 | 3.4 | 97.4 | 98.3 | 0.9 |
| 50-54 | 96.8 | 96.3 | -0.5 | 97.2 | 96.6 | -0.6 |
| 55-59 | 98.4 | 94.2 | -4.2 | 95.7 | 94.5 | -1.2 |
| 60-64 | 94.6 | 89.8 | -4.8 | 91.0 | 89.9 | -1.1 |
| 65 and over | 90.1 | 80.5 | -9.6 | 82.3 | 83.8 | 1.5 |

Table 4.  AVERAGE PERCENTAGE UNDERSTATEMENT OF UNADJUSTED CPS ESTI-
MATES RELATIVE TO INDEPENDENT CURRENT ESTIMATES FOR THE
CIVILIAN NONINSTITUTIONAL POPULATION 14 YEARS OF AGE
AND OVER, BY COLOR AND SEX:  EACH YEAR, 1958–1966

(A minus sign (–) indicates that CPS exceeds
the independent estimate.)

| Year | Nonwhite | | White | | Total Population |
|------|------|--------|------|--------|------------|
| | Male | Female | Male | Female | |
| 1958–1966 | 5.1 | 0.4 | 2.6 | 1.2 | 1.9 |
| 1958 | 4.0 | –0.6 | 2.1 | 0.7 | 1.4 |
| 1959 | 4.9 | –0.6 | 2.5 | 0.9 | 1.6 |
| 1960 | 7.7 | 1.5 | 1.5 | * | 1.1 |
| 1961 | 5.4 | 2.2 | 1.1 | –0.4 | 0.6 |
| 1962 | 6.7 | 1.7 | 2.1 | 1.0 | 1.8 |
| 1963 | 6.5 | 1.6 | 2.7 | 1.5 | 2.2 |
| 1964 | 3.4 | –0.3 | 3.0 | 1.7 | 2.3 |
| 1965 | 4.4 | –0.4 | 4.0 | 2.5 | 3.1 |
| 1966 | 3.2 | –1.4 | 4.0 | 2.6 | 3.0 |

* Percent between –0.05 and +0.05.

Table 5.  AVERAGE PERCENTAGE UNDERSTATEMENT OF UNADJUSTED CPS ESTIMATES
RELATIVE TO INDEPENDENT CURRENT ESTIMATES OF CIVILIAN NON-
INSTITUTIONAL POPULATION, FOR "CONTROL" AGE GROUPS,
BY COLOR AND SEX:  APRIL 1962–DECEMBER 1966.

(A minus sign (–) denotes an excess of CPS over
independent estimate.)

| Year | Nonwhite | | White | | Total Population[1] |
|---|---|---|---|---|---|
| | Male | Female | Male | Female | |
| All ages, 14 and over | 4.9 | 0.2 | 3.3 | 2.0 | 2.6 |
| 14–15 | -1.5 | -4.2 | -2.1 | 0.8 | -1.0 |
| 16–17 | -1.7 | 2.8 | -2.3 | 2.3 | 0.1 |
| 18–19 | 7.4 | 5.2 | 2.3 | 4.4 | 3.8 |
| 20–24 | 19.0 | 6.9 | 7.7 | 4.6 | 6.8 |
| 25–29 | 6.0 | 3.1 | 4.1 | 2.0 | 3.2 |
| 30–34 | 7.2 | 0.6 | 3.8 | 1.3 | 2.6 |
| 35–39 | 5.3 | -4.2 | 3.0 | 0.6 | 1.6 |
| 40–44 | 4.0 | -2.6 | 1.4 | 0.3 | 0.8 |
| 45–49 | 6.4 | -0.5 | 3.6 | 0.7 | 2.2 |
| 50–54 | 0.2 | 0.6 | 3.2 | 0.9 | 1.9 |
| 55–59 | 2.4 | 2.0 | 4.0 | 2.4 | 3.1 |
| 60–64 | 3.9 | -4.9 | 6.2 | 4.3 | 4.7 |
| 65–69 | -13.0 | -23.1 | 2.9 | 0.2 | -0.1 |
| 70 and over | 5.7 | 8.0 | 4.4 | 3.2 | 4.0 |

[1]Computed as the weighted average of sex-color specific percentages with the civilian noninstitutional population, as of July 1, 1964,
at each age, as weights.

Table 6.   ANNUAL ESTIMATES OF THE PERCENTAGE NET UNDERSTATEMENT OF THE
POPULATION 14 YEARS AND OVER, BY COLOR, IN THE CURRENT POPU-
LATION ESTIMATES (SERIES P-25 AND P-20) AND IN UNADJUSTED
CURRENT POPULATION SURVEY ESTIMATES:   1960-1965

(Percentages for each age are additive since in all cases the
percentages are based on the corrected population.   A minus
sign (-) denotes an understatement in the current estimate
in relation to the Current Population Survey.)

| Color and Year | Male | | | Female | | |
|---|---|---|---|---|---|---|
| | Total Understatement of CPS[1] | Understatement of CPS Relative to Current Estimate[2] | Understatement of Current Estimate Relative to Corrected Population[3] | Total Understatement of CPS[1] | Understatement of CPS Relative to Current Estimate[2] | Understatement of Current Estimate Relative to Corrected Population[3] |
| Nonwhite | | | | | | |
| 1960 | 20.1 | 6.7 | 13.4 | 10.9 | 1.3 | 9.6 |
| 1961 | 18.0 | 4.7 | 13.3 | 11.5 | 2.0 | 9.5 |
| 1962 | 19.0 | 5.8 | 13.2 | 11.0 | 1.6 | 9.4 |
| 1963 | 18.8 | 5.7 | 13.1 | 10.8 | 1.4 | 9.4 |
| 1964 | 16.0 | 3.0 | 13.0 | 9.0 | -0.3 | 9.3 |
| 1965 | 16.8 | 3.9 | 12.9 | 8.8 | -0.4 | 9.2 |
| White | | | | | | |
| 1960 | 4.5 | 1.5 | 3.0 | 1.7 | * | 1.7 |
| 1961 | 4.1 | 1.1 | 3.0 | 1.3 | -0.4 | 1.7 |
| 1962 | 5.1 | 2.1 | 3.0 | 2.7 | 1.0 | 1.7 |
| 1963 | 5.7 | 2.6 | 3.1 | 3.2 | 1.5 | 1.7 |
| 1964 | 6.0 | 2.9 | 3.1 | 3.4 | 1.7 | 1.7 |
| 1965 | 7.0 | 3.9 | 3.1 | 4.2 | 2.5 | 1.7 |

*   Percent between +0.05 and -0.05.

[1]   $\dfrac{\text{Corrected population - CPS}}{\text{Corrected population}}$ .

[2]   $\dfrac{\text{Current estimate - CPS}}{\text{Corrected population}}$ .

[3]   $\dfrac{\text{Corrected population - current estimate}}{\text{Corrected population}}$ .

Table 7. ESTIMATED PERCENTAGE NET UNDERSTATEMENT OF THE POPULATION 14 YEARS AND OVER, BY AGE, SEX, AND COLOR, IN THE CURRENT POPULATION ESTIMATES (SERIES P-25 AND P-20) AND IN UNADJUSTED CURRENT POPULATION SURVEY ESTIMATES: 1965

(Percentages for each age are additive since in all cases the percentages are based on the corrected population. A minus sign (-) denotes an understatement in the current estimate in relation to the Current Population Survey.)

| Age and Color | Male | | | Female | | |
|---|---|---|---|---|---|---|
| | Total Understatement of CPS[1] | Understatement of CPS Relative to Current Estimate[2] | Understatement of Current Estimate Relative to Corrected Population[3] | Total Understatement of CPS[1] | Understatement of CPS Relative to Current Estimate[2] | Understatement of Current Estimate Relative to Corrected Population[3] |
| **NONWHITE** | | | | | | |
| Total, 14 and over | 16.8 | 3.9 | 12.9 | 8.8 | -0.4 | 9.2 |
| 14-19 | 7.3 | 2.1 | 5.2 | 5.2 | 0.9 | 4.3 |
| 20-24 | 30.1 | 18.1 | 12.0 | 16.5 | 6.8 | 9.7 |
| 25-29 | 20.9 | 3.5 | 17.4 | 11.7 | 1.9 | 9.8 |
| 30-34 | 23.7 | 3.6 | 20.1 | 8.3 | -0.8 | 9.1 |
| 35-39 | 22.6 | 4.1 | 18.5 | 2.3 | -3.9 | 6.2 |
| 40-44 | 18.1 | 3.5 | 14.6 | 0.2 | -6.1 | 6.3 |
| 45-49 | 15.8 | 2.6 | 13.2 | 6.0 | -0.5 | 6.5 |
| 50-54 | 13.0 | 0.1 | 12.9 | 9.6 | 0.8 | 8.8 |
| 55-59 | 18.5 | -1.3 | 19.8 | 20.5 | 1.1 | 19.4 |
| 60-64 | 13.3 | 6.5 | 6.8 | 7.2 | -3.6 | 10.8 |
| 65 and over | 6.4 | * | 6.4 | 13.4 | -2.6 | 16.0 |

(continued.)

Table 7 (<u>continued</u>).

| Age and Color | Male | | | Female | | |
|---|---|---|---|---|---|---|
| | Total Under-statement of CPS[1] | Under-statement of CPS Relative to Current Estimate[2] | Under-statement of Current Estimate Relative to Corrected Population[3] | Total Under-statement of CPS[1] | Under-statement of CPS Relative to Current Estimate[2] | Under-statement of Current Estimate Relative to Corrected Population[3] |
| WHITE | | | | | | |
| Total, 14 and over | 7.0 | 3.9 | 3.1 | 4.2 | 2.5 | 1.7 |
| 14–19 | 2.8 | 0.2 | 2.6 | 3.1 | 1.5 | 1.6 |
| 20–24 | 10.9 | 7.4 | 3.5 | 7.8 | 5.6 | 2.2 |
| 25–29 | 9.2 | 5.3 | 3.9 | 6.0 | 3.5 | 2.5 |
| 30–34 | 9.3 | 5.3 | 4.0 | 2.8 | 1.4 | 1.4 |
| 35–39 | 6.8 | 3.3 | 3.5 | 2.7 | 1.8 | 0.9 |
| 40–44 | 4.3 | 1.9 | 2.4 | * | 0.3 | -0.3 |
| 45–49 | 6.7 | 4.7 | 2.0 | 1.0 | 1.1 | -0.1 |
| 50–54 | 6.0 | 4.2 | 1.8 | 4.3 | 3.7 | 0.6 |
| 55–59 | 8.0 | 4.2 | 3.8 | 6.9 | 2.7 | 4.2 |
| 60–64 | 7.5 | 6.9 | 0.6 | 6.4 | 4.6 | 1.8 |
| 65 and over | 8.7 | 3.7 | 5.0 | 5.7 | 2.3 | 3.4 |

* Percent between +0.05 and −0.05.

[1] $\dfrac{\text{Corrected population} - \text{CPS}}{\text{Corrected population}}$ .

[2] $\dfrac{\text{Current estimate} - \text{CPS}}{\text{Corrected population}}$ .

[3] $\dfrac{\text{Corrected population} - \text{current estimate}}{\text{Corrected population}}$ .

Table 8.  PERCENTAGE DISTRIBUTION OF THE POPULATION BY COLOR:
APRIL 1, 1967, 1960, AND 1950

(Total resident population for 1950 and 1960;
total population including Armed Forces
overseas for 1967.)

| Color | 1967 | | 1960 | | 1950 | |
|---|---|---|---|---|---|---|
| | Uncor-rected | Cor-rected | Uncor-rected | Cor-rected | Uncor-rected | Cor-rected |
| Total | 100.0 | 100.0 | 100.0 | 100.0 | 100.0 | 100.0 |
| Nonwhite | 12.0 | 12.8 | 11.4 | 12.2 | 10.7 | 11.6 |
| White | 88.0 | 87.2 | 88.6 | 87.8 | 89.3 | 88.4 |

Table 9.  PERCENTAGE CHANGE IN THE WHITE AND NONWHITE POPULATION BY
BROAD AGE GROUPS:  JULY 1, 1960-1965, AND APRIL 1, 1950-1960

(Figures for 1960-1965 relate to total population including
Armed Forces overseas.  Figures for 1950-1960 relate to
total resident population.)

| Period and Age Group | Nonwhite | | White | |
|---|---|---|---|---|
| | Uncorrected | Corrected | Uncorrected | Corrected |
| **1960-1965** | | | | |
| All ages | +12.1 | +10.9 | + 7.1 | + 7.0 |
| 0-4 | + 9.9 | + 2.4 | - 1.3 | - 2.8 |
| 5-14 | +17.3 | +18.6 | + 9.4 | + 9.0 |
| 15-24 | +27.2 | +20.9 | +24.7 | +23.9 |
| 25-34 | - 0.3 | + 0.5 | - 2.7 | - 2.2 |
| 35-44 | + 5.1 | + 6.9 | + 0.4 | + 1.0 |
| 45-54 | + 7.8 | + 3.3 | + 7.0 | + 5.5 |
| 55-64 | +10.0 | +17.0 | + 8.4 | + 8.9 |
| 65 and over | +10.7 | +15.9 | + 8.8 | +10.1 |
| **1950-1960** | | | | |
| All ages | +26.7 | +23.9 | +17.5 | +17.1 |
| 0-4 | +45.5 | +41.8 | +22.2 | +19.2 |
| 5-14 | +52.1 | +46.7 | +44.2 | +44.2 |
| 15-24 | +10.2 | +10.3 | + 7.8 | + 7.8 |
| 25-34 | + 4.9 | + 5.9 | - 5.6 | - 5.7 |
| 35-44 | +11.7 | +10.1 | +11.8 | +11.3 |
| 45-54 | +19.8 | +23.2 | +17.5 | +18.0 |
| 55-64 | +44.4 | +26.9 | +14.7 | +10.7 |
| 65 and over | +37.4 | +37.2 | +34.5 | +38.1 |

Table 10.  INDICES OF DISSIMILARITY FOR SELECTED PAIRS
OF AGE DISTRIBUTIONS

(One-half the sum of the differences in the percentages at each age without regard to sign.)

| Color and Type of Distribution | 1965 | 1960 | 1950 |
|---|---|---|---|
| Nonwhite uncorrected--nonwhite corrected | 2.0 | 1.6 | 1.2 |
| White uncorrected--white corrected | 0.4 | 0.2 | 0.6 |
| Nonwhite uncorrected--white uncorrected | 9.4 | 8.8 | 7.6 |
| Nonwhite corrected--white corrected | 8.2 | 8.2 | 6.8 |

| | 1960 and 1965 | 1950 and 1960 |
|---|---|---|
| Nonwhite uncorrected | 3.1 | 7.0 |
| Nonwhite corrected | 3.7 | 5.8 |
| White uncorrected | 3.1 | 5.2 |
| White corrected | 3.0 | 5.4 |


Table 11.  MEDIAN AGE OF THE POPULATION, BY COLOR:
1965, 1960, AND 1950

(Total resident population in 1960 and 1950; total
population including Armed Forces overseas in 1965.)

| Color | 1965 | | 1960 | | 1950 | |
|---|---|---|---|---|---|---|
| | Uncor-rected | Cor-rected | Uncor-rected | Cor-rected | Uncor-rected | Cor-rected |
| Nonwhite | 21.6 | 23.1 | 23.5 | 24.3 | 26.0 | 26.4 |
| White | 28.9 | 29.0 | 30.3 | 30.3 | 30.7 | 30.6 |
| Difference | 7.3 | 5.9 | 6.8 | 6.0 | 4.7 | 4.2 |

Table 12. DEPENDENCY RATIOS OF THE NONWHITE AND WHITE POPULATION:
1965, 1960, AND 1950

(Figures for 1960 and 1950 relate to total resident
population; figures for 1965 relate to total
including Armed Forces overseas.)

| Color | 1965 (July 1) | | 1960 (April 1) | | 1950 (April 1) | |
|---|---|---|---|---|---|---|
| | Uncor-rected | Cor-rected | Uncor-rected | Cor-rected | Uncor-rected | Cor-rected |
| Nonwhite | 101.8 | 94.0 | 100.7 | 89.2 | 73.6 | 70.8 |
| White | 81.4 | 80.5 | 79.2 | 80.2 | 67.2 | 63.0 |

Table 13. SEX RATIO OF THE TOTAL NONWHITE AND WHITE POPULATION:
1965, 1960, AND 1950

(Males per 100 females. Figures relate to total
population including Armed Forces overseas.)

| Year | Nonwhite | | White | |
|---|---|---|---|---|
| | Uncorrected | Corrected | Uncorrected | Corrected |
| 1965 (July 1) | 94.8 | 97.4 | 97.5 | 98.6 |
| 1960 (April 1) | 95.1 | 98.0 | 98.2 | 99.4 |
| 1950 (April 1) | 96.6 | 99.9 | 99.6 | 100.7 |

Table 14.  VITAL RATES BY COLOR:  1965, 1960, AND 1950

("Corrected" refers only to use of corrected population.  Births
have been adjusted for underregistration in all years.  Figures
relate to total resident population.  Figures for 1950 relate to
48 States.  Rates per 1,000 population.)

| Rate and Year | Nonwhite | | White | |
|---|---|---|---|---|
| | Uncorrected | Corrected | Uncorrected | Corrected |
| **Crude birth rate** | | | | |
| 1965 | 28.5 | 26.0 | 18.4 | 18.0 |
| 1960 | 33.3 | 30.1 | 22.8 | 22.3 |
| 1950 | 32.4 | 28.7 | 23.0 | 22.4 |
| **Crude death rate** | | | | |
| 1965 | 9.6 | 8.8 | 9.4 | 9.2 |
| 1960 | 10.1 | 9.1 | 9.5 | 9.3 |
| 1950 | 10.9 | 9.7 | 9.4 | 9.2 |
| **Crude rate of natural increase** | | | | |
| 1965 | 18.8 | 17.2 | 9.0 | 8.8 |
| 1960 | 23.2 | 21.0 | 13.3 | 13.1 |
| 1950 | 21.5 | 19.1 | 13.6 | 13.2 |
| **Total fertility rate** | | | | |
| 1965 | 4,018 | 3,685 | 2,809 | 2,754 |
| 1960 | 4,685 | 4,276 | 3,553 | 3,494 |
| 1950 | 3,928 | 3,610 | 2,980 | 2,956 |

# PROCEDURAL DIFFICULTIES IN TAKING PAST CENSUSES IN
# PREDOMINANTLY NEGRO, PUERTO RICAN, AND MEXICAN AREAS

Leon Pritzker and N. D. Rothwell
U. S. Bureau of the Census

## Introduction

We have tampered with our assigned topic by expanding in one area and contracting in another. Our expanded topic includes census-taking problems that affect the entire population, although we shall emphasize the impact of these problems on statistics for Negroes particularly, and for Puerto Ricans and Mexicans mostly by indirection since we have limited knowledge about particular procedural problems for them. In contracting, we shall limit ourselves to problems in data collection that affect counting, although we know these problems are related to and occasionally indistinguishable from problems in collecting accurate age, sex, relationship, income, and other data. We are also aware that we are slighting significant procedural difficulties in other stages of a census such as data processing, which, for example, affects the counts of persons with Spanish surnames or Mexican persons.

## Historical Perspective

Having thus redefined the assignment, let us start with a brief historical review.  George Washington observed the conduct of the

first United States Census in 1790 and commented:

> Returns of the Census have already been made from
> several of the States and a tolerably just estimate
> has been formed now in others, by which it appears
> that we shall hardly reach four millions; but one
> thing is certain our real numbers will exceed,
> greatly, the official returns of them; because the
> religious scruples of some, would not allow them
> to give in their lists; the fears of others that
> it was intended as the foundation of a tax induced
> them to conceal or diminished theirs, and thro'
> the indolence of the people, and the negligence of
> many of the Officers numbers are omitted.[1]

In contrast to George Washington's view, perhaps the most com-

placent attitude toward a census was expressed by the Superintendent

of the Census in 1860, Joseph C. G. Kennedy:

> It is evident that the population in all varieties
> of young and old, male and female, was a present
> and visible fact to the enumerator, with scarce a
> chance of omission. . . .
>
> Fortunately for the interests of statistics, the
> unhappy insurrection which developed itself so soon
> after the eighth decennial enumeration was com-
> pleted, was not the occasion of the detention or
> loss of any of the returns, and we are enabled to
> present a true statement of the condition of the
> population immediately preceding the lamentable
> civil war. . . .[2]

The succeeding Superintendent of the Census in 1870, General

Francis A. Walker, expressed very different and what, for his time,

were unorthodox official opinions:

---

[1] John C. Fitzpatrick, ed., The Writings of George Washington
(Washington, D. C.:  U. S. Government Printing Office, 1939), Vol.
31, p. 329.

[2] Census Office, 8th Census, 1860, Population of the United
States in 1860, pp. iii and xlii.

More of the error inevitably enters, through the in-
adequacy of the provisions of the existing census law,
than is pleasant to contemplate. The protracted system of enumeration is essentially vicious, and it is
not possible to cure the evil by any course of administrative treatment. . . .

Now where the enumeration of a people is extended over
such a period of time, a de facto enumeration is of
course impossible. . . . The most familiar illustra-
tion is that of a ward of a city. The enumeration com-
mencing on the 1st of June, and being protracted until
the 10th of September, a family moving on the 1st of
July or the 1st of August from a portion of a ward not
yet visited by the assistant marshal, into a portion of
another ward where the assistant marshal has already
made his rounds, will of course escape enumeration, unless the head of the family so thoroughly appreciates
the importance of the census as to be at pains to hunt
up the proper person and offer information, some portions of which are never given without considerable reluctance. It is assuming more than is fair, to suppose
that one out of a hundred persons so situated will be
at this trouble to perform a duty necessarily more or
less unpleasant. When it is considered how many thousands of persons in every large city, how many tens of
thousands in a city like New York, not only live in
boarding-houses, but change their boarding-houses at
every freak of fancy or disgust, not to speak of those
who leave under the stress of impecuniosity and therefore are not likely to leave their future address or
advertise their residence, it will be seen how utterly
unfitted is such a system of enumeration to the social
conditions of the country at the present time. . . .[3]

In General Walker's complaints about the "essential viciousness

of a protracted enumeration" he touched on a number of problems re-

lated to the fact that a primary use of census statistics is for po-

litical apportionment. Hence, people are supposed to be enumerated

as if they remained in what was their usual residence at the time of

the start of the census. That place becomes less easily determined

---

[3] Census Office, 9th Census, 1870, Vol. I., The Statistics of the
Population of the United States, pp. xxi-xxii.

for mobile people as the enumeration continues beyond the official date, and, furthermore, the possibility of omissions and double enumerations of persons increases.

Although General Washington's and General Walker's views were rare exceptions, they provide historical background for a number of current ideas. First, enumeration of what General Walker referred to as impecunious people in cities has always been difficult, regardless of their particular ethnic or racial identification. Second, sources of difficulties are multiple and interrelated: some difficulties are contributed by the nature of the population to be enumerated--the living arrangements, mobility, and attitudes; some can be attributed to failures of the staff responsible for taking the census; some are related to the nature of the inquiries, the types of questions, and their formulation; others arise from the nature of the task to be completed--a count made as of a fixed date and based on the usual residence of each inhabitant.

These current ideas are in sharp contrast to the one prevailing in the nineteenth century that census statistics are correct by definition. That view is illustrated in the following quotation about the Census of 1900:

> The population of the area of enumeration, June 1, 1900, according to the Twelfth Census was 76,303,387. A careful census is like a decision by a court of last resort-- there is no higher or equal authority to which to appeal. Hence there is no trustworthy means of determining the degree of error to which a census count of population is exposed, or the accuracy with which any particular census is taken. . . .[4]

---

[4] Census Office, 12th Census, 1900, Special Reports: Supplementary Analysis and Derivative Tables, p. 16.

## Post-Enumeration Surveys

For a long time the assumption of correctness precluded critical inquiry by the Census Bureau itself about the accuracy of its own procedures. There was, however, some independent investigation by demographers, including some at the Bureau during the 1930's and 1940's. Yet, it was not until 1950, after the development of sampling theory, techniques, and procedures during the preceding decades, that the Bureau officially took a major step toward discarding the assumption of correctness in census statistics. Sampling theory contributed theories of errors and recognition of errors by users of statistics. More importantly, sampling provided a tool for measuring the accuracy of census data.

Planners of the 1950 sample Post-Enumeration Survey (PES), like their predecessors, assumed that census methodology was basically sound but recognized that there might be some flaws in execution. They believed that the traditional system of having enumerators conduct a canvass and interview in every household required improvement but they did not believe that it required radical change. Their initial hypotheses were that shortcomings of census field procedures, and consequent inaccuracies in the enumeration, were due to some poorly qualified enumerators who were inadequately trained, paid piecework wages, rushed through their assignments with insufficient supervision, who had to interview with less than ideal questionnaires, and who often accepted secondhand information from a housewife about other household members.

Accordingly, the PES was undertaken "to evaluate the coverage and accuracy of responses obtained in the census."[5]   A sample of areas was recanvassed in a search for living quarters missed in the census enumeration.   A second sample consisted of living quarters enumerated in the census which were then re-enumerated.   Consistent with hypotheses about sources of error, the following features were incorporated in the reinterviews:

1.   The PES population information was obtained whenever possible from the "best" respondent, even if this involved repeated call-backs.   Information on personal characteristics for an adult was to be obtained from the person himself, whereas in the census information for all members of a household was obtained from any responsible member of the household who happened to be at home when the enumerator called.

2.   For several items, the PES made use of detailed "probing" questions, in contrast to the more summary form of questions used in the census.

3.   Superior interviewers were selected, and given more intensive training and closer supervision than was possible for the 140,000 enumerators used in the census.

4.   The PES interviewers were paid hourly rates, instead of the piece rates used in the census.

5.   The PES information was compared with the census information on a case-by-case basis by the PES interviewer in the field, immediately following the PES interview.   An explanation of any discrepancies was sought from the respondent, and appropriate changes made in the reinterview results where needed.[6]

The intensive procedures employed for the PES made it cost roughly

[5]Morris H. Hansen and Leon Pritzker,   "The Post-Enumeration Survey of the 1950 Census of Population:   Some Results, Evaluation and Implications."   Paper presented at the Annual Meeting of the Population Association of America, Ann Arbor, Michigan, May 1956 (unpublished; reproduced as PES Results Memorandum No. 54).

[6]U. S. Bureau of the Census, "The Post-Enumeration Survey: 1950," Bureau of the Census, Technical Paper No. 4 (Washington, D. C., 1960).

20 times as much per person as the original Census enumeration. Yet, results measured against bench marks of demographic analysis, like those presented by J. S. Siegel (in his paper in this volume), appear to have shown that the PES had uncovered only about 40 percent of the net underenumeration--that is, less than half of the difference between the "true" count and the Census count. The words "appear to have shown" are used here because it is possible that the estimation procedure introduced a bias, which resulted in an underestimate of the number of persons found in the PES who should legitimately have been included in the census.[7]

Estimates from the PES were that approximately 3.4 million persons, or 2.5 percent of the population, had been erroneously omitted and 1.3 million persons, amounting to about 1.0 percent of the population, had been erroneously included in the 1950 Census. Thus, the net

--------

[7] The PES provided estimates of the difference between the true count of the population and the enumerated count by age, sex, color, etc. The estimates are algebraic sums of two component estimates-- persons missed in the census and persons erroneously enumerated. It has not been feasible to obtain unbiased estimates of these components for the United States as a whole because of the enormous difficulties of searching and matching against an entire census. Our procedure has been to match only against the records of the enumeration district in which an error was alleged to have occurred. Thus we have counted a person as missed if he was not enumerated in the district in which he should have been, even though he was enumerated somewhere else. We have counted a person as overenumerated if he was counted in the district in which he should not have been counted, even though he was not enumerated anywhere else. The algebraic sum of the component estimates made on this basis would give an unbiased estimate of the net difference between the census count and the true count, provided that a completely consistent view was taken of the people who were enumerated once but in the "wrong" enumeration district. We believe that the procedure we adopted did not result in a completely consistent approach, and that the resulting bias was in the direction of understating the net census undercount. This matter is being investigated further.

undercount measured by the survey was about 2 million persons, or 1.5 percent, while the estimates based on demographic analysis showed an undercount of about 3.5 percent for 1950. Although the PES indicated that the Census was more likely to have missed nonwhite than white persons--it showed a 3.3 percent undercount for nonwhites as compared with 1.2 percent for whites--the age-sex-color distributions obtained by the survey closely resembled those of the census. The same relatively high deficiencies of young nonwhite males that existed in the census age-sex-color distributions also existed in the PES statistics.

Our explanation for what might be viewed as a failure of improved execution of traditional data collection techniques to reveal the extent of the census undercount indicates much about the nature and source of the failure:

There are two ways in which people can be missed in a census. One occurs when a building, apartment, or other living quarter is missed. The people who occupy that space are missed as a consequence. The second occurs when all the living space is enumerated but not all of the occupants--either because the enumerators or respondents are confused by the application of residence rules or the definition of a household, or because respondents deliberately withhold information, or because, as we shall see later, they are poorly informed.

Analysis showed that the PES was very successful in finding space that the original census enumerator had missed but was much less effective in uncovering

missed persons--those residing in previously enumer-

ated space who were unreported and those without any

clearly recognizable place of residence.

The evidence for this generalization was not as firm for 1950 as

it subsequently has become, because there was some question about the

effect of timing of the 1950 PES on its results. The survey was con-

ducted three or four months after the census enumeration, and its

failure to identify persons who should have been but were not enumer-

ated can be attributed to the time lag. In 1960, however, a post-

enumeration survey was conducted much closer to the census date and

similar results were observed.

In 1960, as in 1950, the post-enumeration survey estimates of

census undercounts, particularly for nonwhite people, fell short of

those indicated by demographic analysis.[8] The 1960 survey estimates

were that the net deficiency in the count of white persons was 1.6

percent and of nonwhites 3.8 percent, as contrasted with demographic

analysis estimates of undercoverage of 2.2 percent for whites and

10.5 percent for nonwhites.[9] Again, re-enumeration was more success-

---

[8]In 1960, however, the estimate of underenumeration of white females from the post-enumeration survey of 1.7 percent was almost identical with the estimate of 1.6 percent based on demographic analysis.

[9]Eli S. Marks and Joseph Waksberg, "Evaluation of Coverage in
the 1960 Census of Population through Case-by-Case Checking," Proceedings of the Social Statistics Section, American Statistical Association (1966), pp. 62-70. Jacob S. Siegel and Melvin Zelnik, "An
Evaluation of Coverage in the 1960 Census of Population by Techniques
of Demographic Analysis and by Composite Methods," Proceedings of the
Social Statistics Section, American Statistical Association (1966),
pp. 71-85 (this paper is reproduced in the appendix to the present
volume.

ful in identifying missed living quarters than missed persons within already enumerated quarters. A little more than half of those identified as missed in the 1960 Census were in missed living quarters. Other noteworthy similarities between the 1960 and 1950 results that are pertinent to the identification of procedural difficulties might be mentioned. Re-enumeration results showed that census enumerators tended to miss a higher proportion of living quarters in rural areas and in cities with a population of more than a million than they did in suburbs, smaller cities, and towns.[10] They also indicated that persons loosely attached to households, members of the extended family and nonrelatives, were more likely than the head of household, wife, or children to be missed in the census. "Lodgers" showed a particularly high rate of net deficiency.[11]

Some new analysis has shown that a previously suspected source of underenumeration within households was, in fact, responsible for a disproportionate amount of it. This was from what are called "close-out cases," households to which enumerators were not able to gain access even after an initial call and two call-backs. In 1960 such households amounted to about 3 percent of all households in the United States as a whole but 5 percent in cities of 50,000 or more. Enumerators went back to these households to learn what they could from neighbors, janitors, or other people about the number of occupants

---

[10]U. S. Bureau of the Census, "Housing Unit Coverage Errors by Type of Geographic Areas - 1960 Census" (Unpublished Memoranda, 1967).

[11]Unpublished tabulations in Statistical Methods Division files, Bureau of the Census; Bureau of the Census, Technical Paper No. 4, op. cit., p. 9.

and their ages, sex, and color.[12]   A recent tabulation of 1960 results indicates that more than a third of the people identified in the post-enumeration survey as having been missed in enumerated households were in those completed by the closeout procedure.[13]

## The Nature of the Differential Underenumeration of White and Nonwhite Persons in Censuses

Now, we should like to present some conjectures about the nature and sources of errors in census statistics.  The first of these requires an assumption that demographic analyses by Siegel and Zelnik, which provide what we currently consider to be the best estimates of coverage error in total and by color, constitute an acceptable bench mark.  An additional assumption, which has been evaluated and found acceptable, is that the post-enumeration surveys have provided reasonably accurate estimates, by color, of persons missed in the censuses because their living quarters were missed.  The difference between the total underenumeration as measured by demographic analysis and the underenumeration contributed by missed living quarters represents an approximation to the number of persons who were not reported as household members in enumerated private homes; not reported on rosters of places classified as special dwellings, such as rooming houses; not reported in transient quarters such as missions; not reported in in-

---

[12]U. S. Bureau of the Census, U. S. Censuses of Population and Housing, 1960:  Enumeration Time and Cost Study (Washington, D. C., 1963), Table 18, p. 33.

[13]U. S. Bureau of the Census, "Within Household Population Coverage Errors" (Memorandum from Joseph Waksberg to members of the Task Force on Coverage Evaluation, February 9, 1967).

stitutions such as hospitals or jails; and, possibly, who were not staying in any category of places covered by a census enumeration.

The results of this computation, which are shown in Table 1, are dramatic. Seven out of ten white persons but fewer than three out of ten nonwhites who were missed in the 1960 Census were subsequently found in missed quarters by post-enumeration survey interviewers.[14] Thus, a minority of white people but a large majority of nonwhites who were missed in 1960 were either present but unreported in enumerated living quarters or were not staying in any kind of place covered by the census. In addition to conventional housing units, the kinds of places enumerated in the census and covered by the post-enumeration survey in 1960 included housing units in trailers, tents, and houseboats, as well as group quarters and transient accommodations. Examples of the latter two categories are boarding and rooming houses, hotels, motels, barracks, convents, missions, flop houses, jails, reformatories, dormitories, orphanages, and other similar places which have living facilities.[15] There was, however, no attempt to enumerate in places where there were no living facilities; that is, on trains, buses, or planes; in stations, depots, or airports; in hallways, all-night movies, automobiles, abandoned or boarded-up houses; or in other sites not considered habitable. When, therefore, we speak about the

---

[14]Missing housing units was not, however, a trivial cause of underenumeration for nonwhites. Note that Table 1 shows that an estimated 2.5 percent of the nonwhite population as compared with 1.6 percent of white persons were in housing units which the 1960 Census enumerators missed.

[15]Special procedures were used in 1950 and 1960 in an attempt to improve enumeration in transient quarters.

people in the third column of Table 1 as a residual group not found in living quarters missed by census enumerators, we cannot distinguish missed persons in quarters which were enumerated from missed persons who were not present in any living facility covered by the census.

Although the analysis of closeout cases described earlier was not made separately by color of occupant, the potential effect of the closeout procedure, which applied only to identified or enumerated households, appears to be greater for nonwhites than for whites.

The post-enumeration surveys have been too small to provide the kinds of analytical tabulations that would pinpoint communities, neighborhoods, or racial or ethnic groups within communities among which coverage errors are particularly prevalent. Some historical evidence presented in Table 2 is consistent, however, with the hypothesis that underenumeration of Negro males is disproportionately concentrated in urban areas.

In a review of the figures shown in Table 2, an extension of the conjecture presented in Table 1 is relevant: when entire households are missed in a census, the proportions of males and females as expressed in sex ratios are not likely to be affected; but when household rosters are incomplete or when other kinds of living arrangements have not been completely enumerated, it is plausible that the sex ratios would be affected. Thus, the lower sex ratio for Negroes than for native whites is consistent with the PES finding that underenumeration of nonwhites is, to a greater extent than for whites, a missed-persons rather than a missed-households phenomenon. Although the lower sex ratio for Negroes is also consistent with observed differences in sex ratios at birth[16] and presumed differential mortality by sex and color, our conjecture about the effect of underenumeration is reinforced by a study of sex ratios for the age group 20-44. In 1960 the sex ratio based on census statistics for whites aged 20-44 was 97.1, and for Negroes in the same age group it was 87.1, a difference we believe to be greater than might be expected on the basis of demographic factors.

Table 2 also shows that a low sex ratio has been historically an urban phenomenon both for native whites and for Negroes. Although the observed consistently low urban sex ratios for whites as well as for Negroes may result from differential migration of women to cities, our conjecture is that relatively high underenumeration of males in urban areas also contributes to it. At any rate, it is clear that the observed decline in combined urban and rural Negro sex ratios, as measured, can be entirely accounted for by the rapid urbanization of the Negro population. Standardization based on the 1900 Census proportions of rural and urban population produces nearly identical sex ratios in every decade from 1900 to 1960. As much as was available of the kind of data shown in Table 2 was examined region by region to be sure that what have been described here as urban-rural differences were not North-South differences.[17]

---

[16] At birth the sex ratio of whites in the period 1940-1962 was 105.7 and of nonwhites was 102.3 according to Vital Statistics of the United States, Volume 1, 1962, Tables 1-15.

[17] Although in the early decades of the twentieth century the Negro urban sex ratios were particularly low in the South, this regional difference disappeared in the 1950's and 1960's, but the urban-rural differences have persisted.

Sex ratios have also been computed for the age group 20-44

## Other Sources of Information about Procedural Problems

Two or three other bits of information about problems in the conduct of past censuses provide some support for the hypothesis suggested by the historical sex ratios that difficulties in enumerating the Negro population are more city-centered than rural. The sources of the information are the Enumeration Time and Cost Study from the 1960 Census, the procedural histories of the 1950 and 1960 Censuses, and reports of on-the-scene observers.

In the Enumeration Time and Cost Study in 1960, comparisons were made among cities of 50,000 or more, smaller cities, and rural areas. Tables in the published report of that study show that people in large cities are harder to find at home and, as a group, appear to be somewhat less cooperative than people in smaller communities. Six percent of the households in large cities and 3 percent in smaller cities and rural areas required three or more visits to complete enumeration. Five percent of the households in large cities and 2 percent in small cities and rural areas were completed by closeout procedure—that is, information had to be obtained from neighbors or others. Questionnaires containing sample information for the census were mailed back by seven out of ten large-city households and eight out of ten smaller-city and rural households, which resulted in slower

---

covering the period 1910-1960. They follow the pattern of urban-rural differences described here but, unlike the ratios for all ages combined, the urban ratios for whites and Negroes aged 20-44 declined until 1950 and remained nearly constant in 1960. The combined urban-rural sex ratio for this age group of whites and Negroes has also declined since the beginning of the century. The significance of these observations is heightened by the anticipated increase in the proportion of the 20-44 age group in the 1970 and 1980 populations.

completion of the data collection in large cities than elsewhere.[18]

The procedural histories of the 1950 and 1960 Censuses show that, although there was no deliberate planning for differential costs of enumeration, unit costs were higher for the largest Standard Metropolitan Statistical Areas than for other places. The procedural histories also document progress toward reaching General Walker's goal of a fast enumeration. The field canvass for the Census of 1800 took well over a year to complete, while records for 1950 showed that 90 percent of the enumeration was completed within the month of April, and those for 1960 that 98 percent had been enumerated by April 30. In 1960 the remaining 2 percent was not completed until mid-July. Lags were concentrated in New York, Chicago, Los Angeles, and several other large cities.[19] New York and Chicago contained a tenth of all the Negroes and three fourths of all the Puerto Ricans in the United States, while Los Angeles contained 8 percent of the persons with Spanish surnames. Thus, the lags, which were also accompanied by large staff turnover and attendant difficulties, could have had a greater impact on the statistics for Negroes, Puerto Ricans, and Mexicans than for whites.[20]

---

[18] U. S. Bureau of the Census, U. S. Censuses of Population and Housing, 1960: Enumeration Time and Cost Study (Washington, D. C., 1963), Tables 16, 18, p. 33; Table 19, p. 34; Table 26, p. 37; Table 34, p. 41.

[19] U. S. Bureau of the Census, U. S. Censuses of Population and Housing, 1960: Procedural History (Washington, D. C.: U. S. Government Printing Office, 1966), p. 64; Table 9, p. 359.

[20] U. S. Bureau of the Census, U. S. Census of Population: 1960, Subject Reports: Persons of Spanish Surname, PC(2)-1B; Nonwhite Persons by Race, PC(2)-1C; Puerto Ricans in the U. S., PC(2)-1D. (For the sake of comparison, the percentage of the total U. S. population in New York City in 1960 was 4 percent; in Chicago, 2 percent; and in Los Angeles, 1 percent.)

In the cities where lags were greatest and enumerator turnover highest, the Bureau sent staff members to observe and assist _after_ the bulk of the enumeration for the 1960 Census had been completed. At that time, these observers reported that many of the people remaining to be enumerated were either inaccessible (that is, they were rarely at home or were unwilling to answer their door) or they were uncooperative.

## Constraints on Interpretation

We have presented measurements of errors which indicate that nonwhites--who, of course, are principally Negroes--are less completely enumerated than white people. We also have data from the 1950 PES which indicate that census coverage among poor uneducated people is not as good as among the more affluent or educated; and Negroes, Puerto Ricans, and Mexicans certainly have been overrepresented among the poor and uneducated.

We have also cited evidence that troubles in taking a census-- troubles which historically have been linked with errors--are more prevalent in the largest cities of the United States and the cities where there are high concentrations of Negroes and Puerto Ricans. Although we _believe_ that there is a connection between the errors measured and the problems described, our evidence is not definitive. Thus, we have conjectures and not conclusions.

Experience with a different coverage problem may explain such caution: In 1940 a match of the Census results with birth records indicated considerable underenumeration of infants. The presumption was that people did not think of their infants as household members or, if they did, it was in some special most-easily-forgotten category. In 1950 a similar match was performed, but follow-up inquiries revealed that 80 percent of the times that babies were missed their parents were also. Hence, the problem was not, as originally thought, the underreporting of infants per se but the missing of entire families in which infants were present. Improved questions about babies would have been no solution for the redefined problem. It called for more thorough canvassing techniques.

By analogy, we might now incorrectly assume that the kinds of problems described in observers' reports were the predominant causes of census errors when, in fact, we had overlooked some places like bus depots, subways, hallways, and all-night movies which had not even been canvassed; or had depended on incomplete counts from nonprivate housing-unit sources such as institutions or hotels or missions; or had not seen weaknesses in the rural enumeration; or had failed to note a substantial contribution to error from seemingly cooperative people who, out of misunderstanding or fear, reported incomplete household rosters.

Although fear of enumeration in a census may be unwarranted, it nevertheless is real for people who feel that in divulging the truth they could jeopardize their homes or livelihood. Currently, enumerators tell of respondents who fear to report complete household rosters because public housing authorities or their landlords would evict them for overcrowding. They say that violations of increasingly strict housing codes result in underreporting of lodgers or tenants. They speak of welfare regulations which mitigate against the reporting of wage earners or, in some places, of unemployed men in the home. Public housing, urban codes regulating use of private housing, and the welfare system are all relatively recent developments. Since we believe that undercoverage of the urban population in censuses has been persistent and predates these developments, we must hypothesize the existence of some equivalent historical constraints on full enumeration. Alternatively, we might give more weight to enumerators' reports that fear of local police and other authorities, and what General Walker called "the stresses of impecuniosity" in the guise of credit collectors, affect the census counts. While refusals to be interviewed are straightforward and hostile respondents are obvious, erosion of the census count may be occurring in far less dramatic situations and may often be imperceptible to the most sophisticated enumerators or observers.

## Tests of Methods of Improving Coverage

Although shy about drawing cause-and-effect conclusions, the Census Bureau has conducted many tests of hypotheses about sources of problems and errors. Some have been carefully designed experiments, others merely tests of feasibility, and others have been what might be classified as ad hoc projects arising from the need to cope with an immediate difficulty. Voluminous files describe results of these tests, but only a few tests will be cited as examples.

In connection with a special census in the city of New York in 1957, some experiments were conducted to see whether the procedures employed were responsible for an important part of the undercounts, particularly in slum areas. In the first experiment, three such areas were selected to test the use of neighborhood leaders as enumerators. The distinction sought was between leaders and other residents, not between neighborhood and outside enumerators, since decennial- and special-census staffs are typically recruited from within the communities to be enumerated. The people selected as leaders re-enumerated a sample of apartments in blocks they chose. Comparisons between their results and the original enumeration indicated that the recheck enumerators missed more persons than the original enumerators had.

In connection with the same special census, students in the city schools were required to take a census form home, have it completed by their family, and return it. The results of a matching study between the school forms and census schedules indicated that the school forms could improve coverage; but many clerical errors and double counting, arising from different designations for the same persons, reduced the usefulness of the match. A third test, which involved matching census results with welfare rolls, revealed almost no missed persons.[21]

More procedural tests were made in 1958 in connection with a census in Indianapolis. Five experimental procedures were employed, all of which were postcensus checks on the completeness of the coverage

---

[21]William W. Winnie, Jr., "New York City Special Census, Special Study No. 4, Special Re-enumeration to Evaluate Coverage Within Dwelling Units" (unpublished, October 7, 1957); William W. Winnie, Jr., "New York City Special Census, Special Study No. 3, Sample Survey of the Results of the School Form Program" (unpublished, September 1, 1957); U. S. Bureau of the Census, Statistical Research Division, "The Matching Problem," New York City Special Census - Special Study No. 7 (Matching Households on Relief Designated by New York City against Special Census Schedules, unpublished, September 11, 1957).

obtained by enumerator canvass. In combination, all five procedures

were effective in increasing coverage by little more than 2 percent

for white persons and by nearly 6 percent for nonwhites. The most

effective single procedure was a check made in the post office by

letter carriers to identify residential addresses missed in the cen-

sus. Furthermore, this procedure required the least amount of cleri-

cal work and was the most free of error. It was tested again in other

communities, employed experimentally in the 1960 Census, and provided

the kind of experience that led to current proposals for 1970 Census

procedures.[22]

During the 1960's other procedural tests have been conducted,

and their results are reflected in the plans for the 1970 Census,

which is the subject of another paper. The only results we shall men-

tion, therefore, are those which shed some light on past procedural

difficulties.

In a 1964 test of the effectiveness of employing an address

register to make initial contacts with households by mail instead of

by personal interview, a closeout rate was computed and compared with

the rate for the same neighborhoods in 1960. These were city slum

neighborhoods in Louisville, Kentucky. The test indicated that the

new procedure had reduced by half the proportion of cases where none

of the required census information could be obtained at firsthand from

---

[22] U. S. Bureau of the Census, "Tests of Use of Post Office Re-
sources to Improve Coverage of Censuses," Working Paper No. 19 (1965);
U. S. Bureau of the Census, Statistical Methods Branch, "Summary of
Special Lists, Procedures, and Other Related Results, Indianapolis
Experimental Coverage Procedures Test, Results Memorandum No. 5" (un-
published, February 27, 1958).

anyone in the household.[23]

In the 1964 test in Louisville and again in a 1965 test in Cleveland, Ohio, an address register was compiled on the basis of information cumulated from a commercial list supplier, the post office, and respondents' reports. The mail was then used as the initial data collection agent, followed when necessary by personal contact by an enumerator. In both tests experimental evidence was obtained that coverage of the total white and Negro population, but not of Negro men, had been improved.[24]

## Concluding Remarks

Recent history reinforces optimism that there are reasonable solutions to the past census omissions arising from enumerators' failures to find every building and every living quarter. In a number of tests the Bureau has collected evidence of its ability to improve housing-unit coverage, white and nonwhite. There is also a reasonable expectation of being able, if only by mail, to establish some direct contact with all identifiable households and thus to re-

---

[23]U. S. Bureau of the Census, "Closeout rates in X-2 area ED's, 1960 rates vs. 1964 rates" (memorandum from Ernest Tracey and Barnett Denton to Leon Pritzker, October 30, 1964).

[24]"Population and Housing Coverage in the Cleveland Special Census," Cleveland Special Census Results Memorandum No. 13 (prepared by Statistical Methods Division, October 15, 1965); "More Information on Coverage of Nonwhite Population," Cleveland Special Census Results Memorandum No. 36 (memorandum from Joseph Waksberg to Conrad Taeuber and Morris Hansen, July 19, 1966); "Louisville Evaluation. Population and Occupied Housing Unit Coverage in Missed and Overenumerated Housing Units," Results Memorandum No. 15 (prepared by Statistical Methods Division, August 31, 1964).

duce closeout cases. We are, however, less sanguine about the success of our efforts to find solutions to the problem of enumerating people who for one reason or another are not reported by householders or who are not associated with any particular household or other type of living quarter in which the census is taken.

In the light of achieved completeness of coverage of 97 or 98 percent, a continuing drive for coverage improvement in decennial censuses may appear to be straining for a trivial goal. Yet, levels of achievement which appear impressive on a national level become problematical when viewed in the perspective of demands for small-area data and for data about minority racial and ethnic groups. Striving for improved coverage does not derive from a desire to reach 99.44 percent completion at the national level so much as from the need to work toward uniform coverage of all groups in the population--of Negroes, whose count is known to be deficient, as well as of Puerto Ricans and Mexicans, whose counts we presume are also deficient. Consistent with our view that undercoverage arises from multiple inter-related sources, we are not seeking any panacea but are making many kinds of efforts which now seem plausible and potentially effective for achieving the goal of a more complete census.

Table 1.  COMPUTATIONS INDICATING NATURE OF DIFFERENTIAL UNDER-
ENUMERATION OF WHITE AND NONWHITE PERSONS
IN THE 1960 CENSUS

| Color | Siegel-Zelnik Estimate of Net Underenumeration in 1960 Census[1]<br><br>(1) | Re-enumeration Survey Estimate of Missed Persons in Missed Living Quarters in 1960 Census<br>(2) | Other Missed Persons--Estimated as Difference between (1) and (2)<br>(3) |
|---|---|---|---|
| | Thousands of Persons | | |
| Total | 5,702 | 3,143 | 2,559 |
| White | 3,560 | 2,568 | 992 |
| Nonwhite | 2,142 | 575 | 1,567 |
| | Percentage of Underenumerated Total | | |
| Total | 100.0 | 55.1 | 44.9 |
| White | 100.0 | 72.1 | 27.9 |
| Nonwhite | 100.0 | 26.8 | 73.2 |
| | Percentage of Estimated "True" Total Population[2] | | |
| Total | 3.1 | 1.7 | 1.4 |
| White | 2.2 | 1.6 | 0.6 |
| Nonwhite | 9.5 | 2.5 | 7.0 |

[1]Derived from percentages shown in the paper by Jacob S. Siegel and Melvin Zelnik, "Evaluation of Coverage in the 1960 Census of Population by Techniques of Demographic Analysis and by Composite Methods," Proceedings of the Social Statistics Section, American Statistical Association (1966).

[2]Denominators are published census totals plus the estimates of persons shown in column 1.

Table 2.   SEX RATIOS OF THE NEGRO AND NATIVE-BORN WHITE POPULATION,
BY URBAN-RURAL RESIDENCE:   1820-1960

| Census Year | Negro Population | | | | Native-born White Population | | | |
| | % Urban | Sex Ratio | | | % Urban | Sex Ratio | | |
| | | Total | Urban | Rural | | Total | Urban | Rural |
|---|---|---|---|---|---|---|---|---|
| 1960 | 73 | 93.4 | 90.4 | 101.9 | 68 | 97.5 | 94.5 | 104.4 |
| 1950 | 62 | 94.3 | 90.0 | 101.7 | 63 | 98.6 | 93.6 | 104.7 |
| 1940 | 49 | 95.0 | 88.1 | 102.1 | 55 | 100.1 | 94.5 | 107.5 |
| 1930 | 44 | 97.0 | 91.3 | 101.7 | 54 | 101.1 | 96.0 | 107.6 |
| 1920 | 34 | 99.2 | 95.4 | 101.2 | 50 | 101.7 | 96.9 | 106.7 |
| 1910 | 27 | 98.9 | 90.8 | 102.1 | 44 | 102.7 | 97.3 | 107.1 |
| 1900 | 23 | 98.6 | 87.8 | 102.1 | 39 | 102.8 | 96.9 | 106.6 |
| 1890 | 19 | 99.5 | * | * | 34 | 102.9 | * | * |
| 1880 | * | 97.8 | * | * | * | 102.1 | * | * |
| 1870 | * | 96.2 | * | * | * | 100.6 | * | * |
| 1860 | * | 99.6 | * | * | * | 103.7 | * | * |
| 1850 | * | 99.1 | * | * | * | 103.1 | * | * |
| 1840 | * | 99.5 | * | * | * | 104.6 | * | * |
| 1830 | * | 100.3 | * | * | * | 103.7 | * | * |
| 1820 | * | 103.4 | * | * | * | 103.3 | * | * |

*Not ascertained.


Note:   The principal data for this table were compiled by Nampeo
R. McKenney of the Ethnic Origins Statistics Branch, Population Division, from these sources:   United States Censuses of Population for
1910, 1920, 1930, 1940, 1950, 1960; Negroes in the United States, 1790-
1915; Negroes in the United States, 1920-1932.

# NEEDED INNOVATIONS IN 1970 CENSUS DATA COLLECTION
## PROCEDURES:  A CENSUS VIEW

Conrad Taeuber
Assistant Director
Bureau of the Census


In his testimony before the House Appropriations Subcommittee

on April 5, Census Director, A. Ross Eckler, made the following

statement about plans for the 1970 Census:

> It has become clear that, in the congested areas of
> our large cities, and in rural poverty areas, some
> additional work will be required in order to carry
> out an effective enumeration.  Our evaluation stud-
> ies of the 1960 Census have shown that the propor-
> tion of the population which was missed in that cen-
> sus is especially high among the groups which tend
> to be concentrated in these areas, and there is evi-
> dence that the underenumeration of young Negro men
> was large enough to significantly impair the value
> of the statistics for some uses.  But these are the
> very areas and groups where the need for statistics
> is greatest.  I feel that I would be remiss if I did
> not call this situation to your attention and sug-
> gest that additional efforts should be made to deal
> with these increasingly difficult problems.

As part of his concluding remarks, the Director put a tentative price

tag on the efforts planned for 1970:

> Though I cannot provide a firm cost estimate at this
> time, I believe that the developing situation will
> justify increases in the cost of the 1970 Census over
> and above the cost of repeating the 1960 Census.
> This will probably be in the range of $20 to $25 mil-
> lion, of which about half would be devoted to the ad-
> ditional efforts to improve the enumeration in the
> areas which are especially difficult for census tak-
> ing.

For most of the past year, a Census Bureau Committee has been devoting attention to the problems of "difficult to enumerate" groups in the census. Their work has involved contacts with persons in other federal agencies, universities, private research groups, and community action agencies, as well as other persons with experience with related problems. The Committee has evaluated the experience of the Bureau in special censuses and current surveys, and has developed proposals and field tests.

Plans for the 1970 Census include giving special attention to the groups that may not be reached through the regular efforts. General publicity is an important element in this effort, and we have every reason to believe that the mass media will again be most generous in publicizing the fact that a census is being taken and in urging people to be sure that they are included.

In 1970, the advance mailing in major metropolitan areas will contain the census form itself with a request that it be filled in and returned to the Census Office by mail. In the rest of the country the advance form will be distributed by mail with the request that the answers be supplied and held for the enumerator when he calls.

The direct mailing in the metropolitan areas will be to specific addresses at which people live or might live. A list of such addresses is essential to the control of the field enumeration. Since there is no comprehensive list of this type in the United States, it has been necessary, in the past, for the enumerators to develop such a list as they made their rounds in the designated areas.

In the search for improved means of providing the necessary

list of all residential units, the Bureau considered a number of possibilities. The advent of the computer made it possible to use lists that had been prepared in advance, for the computer could readily rearrange any list in a manner that would make it useful for census purposes. After some testing of alternatives, the Bureau has decided to use a system that relies in the first instance on commercially prepared mailing lists, supplementing these by utilizing the knowledge of the mail carriers who serve the area. In the city mail delivery areas in which the mail-out/mail-back procedure is to be used, the latest available commercial mailing list is to be checked by the Post Office in advance of the census date. Each address on the list is printed on a card. These cards are sorted down to mail carrier routes and then each carrier is given the cards for his route, asked to sort them as though he were to deliver mail to them, to note any nonexistent or incorrect addresses, and to add cards of a distinctive color for every address on his route for which he did not have a card in the set originally given to him. Quality control procedures are used to help assure that this step is properly done. The additions and corrections are then incorporated into the computer list, addresses marked for deletion are removed, and such field checking as is needed at this point is then undertaken.

The lists are used to prepare the mailing pieces, with the proper designation of those addresses to which the longer sample form is to be sent as well as those to which the shorter form is to be sent. The addressed questionnaires are then given to the postal service for normal delivery of mail to the specified addresses. At this point the carrier will be under instructions to prepare a card for any household on his route for which he does not then have an addressed questionnaire. These cards are turned over to the Census Office, the new addresses are added to the register, and the appropriate questionnaire is then mailed to each additional unit. After the mail returns are in, the enumerator is given a copy of the register showing every address that received a long or a short form and indicating which need a follow-up because no return has been received or because the questionnaire that was returned is not fully acceptable. The enumerator is responsible for assuring that there is a fully acceptable return for every address on the list or an appropriate explanation for the missing ones. The enumerators will also have instructions to be alert to any housing units which, despite the previous checking, are improperly included or excluded.

Persons who receive mail as boxholders rather than through the delivery service will be included. Special steps will also have been taken in advance to identify apartments in those multiunit structures in which the separate units do not have a systematic identification such as Apartment 103. Equally important is the assurance that every apartment in a multiunit structure is accounted for on the list. An important feature of this procedure is that the enumerator has a precise address, that is, Apartment 103 or second floor rear apartment at 1727 Pennsylvania Avenue, N.W. This enables the enumerator and the field supervisor to know whether or not a particular unit has been included. The address must make it possible to find the unit if it is necessary to go there.

The areas to be covered by a mail procedure will include some sections that are not served by city delivery carriers. For these areas, advance lists will be prepared by census enumerators through a field canvass. The location of housing units is to be plotted on maps, and names of household heads will be used where no suitable address can be established. These are then incorporated into the mailing lists.

In most rural areas such addresses are not available and it has not been feasible to develop adequate lists in advance. Addresses such as "Battery Lane," or "third house on the right from the filling station at the crossroads," or "Route 3, Box 121," do not provide the type of address that is needed for census purposes. For administrative reasons, the conventional enumeration procedure is to be used in areas including 35-40 percent of the total national population.

Special procedures will be used to enumerate people who do not live in households but are in institutions, military establishments, in college dormitories, migratory labor camps, hotels, motels, etc. Some people have no fixed place of abode and are to be found only in missions, flop houses, or even all-night movie houses. Special arrangements will be made to enumerate such people. Provisions will also be made to enumerate persons who are away from home at the time of the census, on business, on vacation, or for other reasons, and to have them counted at their usual place of residence. Large rooming houses will be the objects of special attention.

Concern has been expressed that the appeal to fill out and mail the census questionnaires may be met by a very low response rate in areas in which the enumeration under any other method is also difficult. It is recognized that in some of the congested areas of the large cities there will be special problems. Such areas will be identified in advance of the census. In addition, the great bulk of the returned questionnaires are received within a very few days of the census date, and, therefore, areas of low response can quickly be identified. Special enumerator effort can then be concentrated in these areas.

In our tests, the response rates in such areas have been somewhat below those for other parts of the city, but they have been high enough to warrant the use of the mail-out/mail-back procedure. In both Louisville and Cleveland, poverty areas were delineated in advance. In Louisville, the rate of return for the control group in the poverty areas was about 70 percent, compared with almost 90 percent for the remainder of the city. In Cleveland, the comparable response rates were 60 percent and 80 percent.

In major metropolitan areas, additional efforts are being developed for use within the areas in which difficulties of enumeration can be anticipated. Special district offices will be established there to supervise the work and to expedite the review of the questionnaires for acceptability before giving them out to enumerators for follow-up. The enumerators working out of these offices will be under closer supervision than is generally feasible for the majority of the district offices.

Efforts will be made in these areas to enlist the help of community leaders in order to persuade residents that cooperation with the census is not only a matter of civic duty but is directly serving

the interest of the people themselves.

In the tests that have been conducted we have given special at-

tention to the problems in poverty areas.  Public information and

public relations programs are essential components of any census.

We have tried some innovations as well as more intensive use of the

media on which the Bureau normally relies.  Among the special de-

vices used were assistance centers in public schools and posters and

banners on buses and post office trucks.  Radio and television cov-

erage included spot announcements, regular progress reports, an "open

mike" program, and interviews by Census Bureau staff members.  News-

paper coverage included stories, features, photographs, and editori-

als.  School children took home flyers urging cooperation in the cen-

sus, and in some churches public announcements were made.  In a fol-

low-up survey we found that newspapers and television were most fre-

quently credited as the main source of information about the census

before the form itself was received.

In New Haven, we have secured lists of high school dropouts and

of persons seeking employment through local Community Action Agencies.

In cooperation with the Bureau of Labor Statistics, an effort is being

made to identify persons who are found and interviewed in casual set-

tings, such as on street corners, in poolrooms, and bars.  Individuals

so identified are matched against the census records.  If they are not

found there, a follow-up interview will be conducted to establish

where they should be counted.

In connection with a special census in Memphis recently we sent an advance notice to persons in selected areas informing them that the enumerator would call on a particular day between 4:30 and 8:30 p.m. Enumerators traveled in teams accompanied by a supervisor. They were able to complete their assigned tasks within the time specified.

We have been planning a small-scale intensive test of techniques for dealing with the special problems of census taking in congested areas. This was to be carried out in Philadelphia in the fall of 1967. It incorporates the features which past experience has shown might be most helpful, and these include the following:

1. For the designated areas, training and supervision of temporary field personnel will be on a much more intensive basis than is feasible generally. The ratio of supervisors to enumerators will be increased and there will be much closer supervision of the daily progress of the enumerators.

2. In addition to the regular procedure of establishing a list of addresses and mailing the questionnaires, as elsewhere in the metropolitan areas, there will be a complete recanvass in these areas in an effort to make certain that all housing units have actually been included. There is also to be a recheck on the completeness of the count of persons within households.

3. The census is concerned with counting persons at their usual place of residence. Visitors who state that they are being enumerated elsewhere are not included in the count at the address where they are found. Consideration is being given to a variation of this procedure in the poverty areas, to include all persons who are found at an address, to make provision for the reallocation of these individuals to

the place which they claim as their residence and checking the persons counted at that address to avoid duplication. This procedure could be extended to institutions where individuals usually remain for only short periods of time, to make certain that all of these persons are actually counted at the places of their usual residence. If all persons found at a particular address are to be counted, including those who claim residence elsewhere, it may be necessary to provide assurance that the "visitors" will not be included in the household count at that place.

4. Efforts are also being made to develop intensified public information programs, specifically developed for the groups in the difficult-to-enumerate areas. These include special appeals to enlist the support of the local leadership, efforts to develop word-of-mouth campaigns for the benefit of the census, appeals to the self-interest of the respondents in having the census complete, recognition of the special problems in areas where a foreign language is dominant, the establishment of store front assistance centers that are open in the evenings, and the use of local area personnel as enumerators or as "interpreters." Attention is being given to the simplification of the census questions and instructions.

5. The employment of special crews to work at unusual hours (very early in the morning or late into the evening) is also indicated for some areas.

6. Attention is to be given to rooming houses and other establishments which house people for short periods of time. It has been suggested that in each such establishment the person in charge be em-

ployed as a census enumerator and made responsible for the enumeration of the individuals in the structure on census day.

The problems of undercoverage in rural areas are somewhat different in that there are fewer persons involved in any one area. Efforts have been made to provide the most up-to-date maps available for the assistance of the enumerators. One new procedure under consideration for rural areas involves the use of lists developed by the Post Office as a check on the completeness of the census. In view of the nature of the census procedures in these areas, this would require a check by the Post Office in the field after the enumerators had completed their work. After a matching of the two lists, steps would then be taken to secure census reports for any household identified by the Post Office which was found not to have been included in the census enumeration.

The problems of "difficult to enumerate" groups is not unique to the census. The Bureau has also given special attention to these problems in connection with the Current Population Survey. These involve special training programs for new interviewers and retraining as needed. There is periodic preparation of intensive training materials, including home study exercises, group training to emphasize listing the location of addresses and identification of housing units and probing to assure coverage of all persons in the household. A regular monthly reinterview program assures that a part of the work of each interviewer is checked by another specially trained person several times during the course of a year. Interviewers whose work does not meet the standards of acceptance are identified for retraining and observation or for dismissal. At periodic intervals the reinterview program will concentrate especially on coverage checks. Despite these and other efforts, there is a continuing need to find more effective means of improving the completeness of coverage.

It is difficult to establish a cost-effectiveness analysis of efforts that may be developed for the improvement of the coverage of the census. The Census of Population and Housing as now visualized will cost approximately 70 cents per person enumerated, including the tabulation and publication of results. The marginal cases undoubtedly cost far more. Our tests so far have indicated that some improvement in coverage is to be expected from the overall changes in methods that are being developed. The use of the more intensive procedures outlined would undoubtedly result in a reduction in the amount of undercoverage. At this point one of our needs is for suggestions on the ways in which we could maximize the improvement in relation to the added costs.

# NEEDED IMPROVEMENTS IN CENSUS DATA COLLECTION PROCEDURES
## WITH SPECIAL REFERENCE TO THE DISADVANTAGED

Everett S. Lee
Department of Sociology
University of Massachusetts

Since I have been offering gratuitous advice to the Census Bureau for years, it is not easy for me to come up with a set of recommendations for the 1970 Census that have not already been fully considered. Over the years the Census staff has dealt with me and the various committees of which I have been a member with kindness and patience. They have accepted a number of our recommendations, sometimes to our later embarrassment, and they have shown a commendable willingness to indulge in judicious experimentation. They need no one to tell them that more and better data are needed on the disadvantaged, and only their better judgment or their awareness of financial or other difficulties has kept them from implementing some of our more ambitious proposals.

I therefore have few differences with the Census Bureau when we operate in terms of what appears to be the possible. But I would venture to suggest that the possible may have been too narrowly defined. In order to develop this point it is useful to review the development of the census and to indicate some of the principles upon which it has been based.

Fortunately the decennial census is a constitutional requirement; otherwise it would certainly have fallen victim to an economy-minded administration at some time or other, since it is always easy to rank other needs above the need for information about the number, distribution, and characteristics of our people. It is fair to say that additions to census schedules, tabulations, and publications have always been made grudgingly. This is not entirely a matter of economy—there is always fear that information will be misused, and there is always some question as to when the bounds of propriety are overstepped in the collection of personal data. Who cannot recall the furor aroused by the introduction of a question on income, and who has not participated in the argument over the introduction of a question on religion? Indeed, there is probably no item on the census schedule that has not occasioned some objection. Even the question on age, without which many of the others are pointless, has been vociferously opposed; and I am told, though I cannot document it, that the feminists of the twenties were against the question on sex of respondent on the grounds that it was impertinent and discriminatory.

Nevertheless the Census has grown from the handful of items collected in the first census to the massive accumulation of 1960. Indeed, it can be argued with some merit that the schedule is now so long as to exhaust the tolerance of the respondent, so that for every item added another must be eliminated. It was in part to meet this problem that the great innovation of the 1940 Census was made, the introduction of sampling. A subsequent innovation, the use of the mail questionnaire, made possible by the increasing literacy and sophistication of our population, reduced interviewer time and permitted a more leisurely completion of the schedule. But certain fundamental principles of the census have remained essentially unchanged since 1790. These are:

1. That the census be taken decennially and as of a single date.
2. That the census be completed in a single enumeration for each person.
3. That everyone be exposed to the same series of questions except where manifestly inappropriate; or where sampling is involved, that everyone have an equal chance of being asked a given series of questions.

It can be argued that the first of these principles is dictated by the Constitution; that the second is necessary in order to keep costs down; and that the third is a democratic imperative. I propose, however, that they be re-examined in view of the increasing rapidity of social change and in light of the obvious need for more and different data for some parts of our population than for others.

When the founding fathers provided for a count of the population for the purpose of determining representation, the ten-year interval between censuses seemed quite reasonable. But representation in the Congress is only one of the many purposes for which censuses are now taken. The Census, as its brochures indicate, is the fact finder for the nation, and the acceleration of the rate of social change has increased both the number and the consequences of the decisions that must be made by local as well as state and national governments. California has been chronically underrepresented in the Congress, and the idea of "one man, one vote" will be ineffective unless a more frequent accounting of the population is made. The population of counties and cities can change with startling rapidity. Levittowns rise almost overnight, and the ethnic character of neighborhoods is far from constant.

Current data are, of course, no guarantee of appropriate social action, but that is hardly an argument for handicapping planners in pursuit of their goals. Only censuses can provide adequate data for local areas throughout the country, and ten years is a long time between censuses, as any student of population change in Philadelphia, Chicago, Los Angeles, the nation's capital, or the delta counties of Mississippi will testify. The introduction of the five-year census is long overdue. Why should we continue to take decennial censuses of population? Do we still place knowledge of natural resources above knowledge of human resources? A most important innovation in the data collection procedures of the 1970 Census would be the treatment of this one as the first of a series of five-year censuses; and for no other parts of the population would this be more important than for the Negro, the Puerto Rican, the Indian, and the Mexican American.

Not only should the census be taken more frequently, it should be taken in stages. We have, of course, never taken the census on a single day, but neither have we deviated from the attempt to take it as of a single date. Because of this, we have not been able to use information gathered in the initial stage of the census as a guide for later procedures. If the census could be taken in stages, the initial

data—say the 100 percent items proposed for 1970—could be used to determine the collection of sample data at a later stage.  In other words,
the first and complete enumeration could be used to provide a sampling
frame for a second enumeration, and that for still another, and so on.

Such a procedure, while certainly expensive, could result in
great improvement in the data for minority groups or for small segments
of the population.  For example, present sample data for populations
which are few in number in a given area are sometimes unusable because
of sampling variability.  This is unavoidable with the present system
of sampling, which determines in advance that every "nth" household
or person will be selected for additional questions without regard for
color or ethnic group.  But if data from an initial enumeration were
available, the proportion to be selected in the sample could be varied
and sampling variation reduced.  In some instances the appropriate
sample would be 100 percent, while in others it could be less than the
proportion now taken.  I am not unmindful of the difficulties posed in
the inflation of such a sample, but I have confidence in the ingenuity
of Hansen and his associates and in the capacity of modern computers.

Ideally, this procedure should be followed for the entire Census
of 1970.  Shortage of time and money will doubtless render this too
difficult, but it should not be impossible to implement this procedure
in part.  One of the most promising developments for the 1970 Census
was the proposed $2\frac{1}{2}$ percent sample, to be taken simultaneously with the
other parts of the census and featuring important items that could not
be included in either the full count or the 25 percent sample.  My understanding is that plans for this sample were shelved when a 1968 sur-

vey was projected for some two million persons. Now, unfortunately, the 1968 survey has been eliminated for economic reasons, and the $2\frac{1}{2}$ percent sample is the major possibility left for obtaining some of the most needed data for 1970. For example, an item proposed for that sample dealt with occupation in 1965, a question that could be linked with the five-year mobility question and used to determine the social mobility of various groups of the population.

As a minimum, therefore, I propose that this sample, or better still a somewhat larger one, be reinstituted. I further suggest that its utility for the study of the disadvantaged be broadened by varying the sampling proportions in accordance with the size of certain groups. This can best be done if the sample follows the regular census, using it as a sampling frame; but it is possible to use knowledge from other sources to improve upon a flat sample, even if taken concurrently. An overall sample of, say, 5 percent is adequate for the country as a whole, for regions, for large cities, and for most states; but it is not adequate for smaller areas, and here too needs are great.

Another departure from conventional procedures, but one that is not completely without parallel, is the provision of separate sets of questions for different groups of people. Again this multiplies the difficulties of the Census Bureau enormously, but the gains would more than justify the added expenditure of funds and effort. Furthermore, the improvement in the ability to take rational action on behalf of the disadvantaged should offset the annoyance caused by such special questions to be asked of Negroes, of Puerto Ricans, or of Mexican Americans.

An example of a question already considered by the Bureau and probably rejected is the tribal identification of the American Indian.

Other questions immediately suggest themselves for the various groups of the disadvantaged, but the only item I shall stress is one dealing with the proper identification of the Mexican American. Without some sort of question on ethnic identification, not only Mexican Americans but other disadvantaged groups are simply not identified in the census. Many attempts have been made in the past, with indifferent success, to identify some of these groups in terms of the individual's birthplace or the birthplace of parents; actually this works fairly well for the first and second generations, but for the third and later generations, an increasingly important group, some other tack is necessary.

Finally we should squarely face the problem of underenumeration. We know practically nothing about the underenumeration of Mexican Americans, Puerto Ricans, and American Indians. In part this is a matter of definition, and it is clear from the results of the 1960 Census that self-identification may differ markedly from the identification assigned by an interviewer—witness the phenomenal increase in the enumerated American Indian population over the decade 1950-1960. It is quite clear that the Negro has been consistently underenumerated. The comparison of the 1940 Census with draft registrations and the various studies of the 1950 and 1960 Censuses offer convincing evidence that considerable numbers of Negro households are missed in the census and that the enumeration of young adult, unattached, Negro males is especially deficient.

It seems clear to me that self-identification on mail questionnaires is a better guide to ethnic group than was afforded by interviewer methods.  This alone raised the level of enumeration of the
American Indian; but other methods are necessary to improve the re-
cording of other groups.  In particular I suggest that some of the
techniques that have been used in underdeveloped countries should be
experimented with in connection with underdeveloped peoples in the
United States.

The areas are well known in which underenumeration is most
serious.  These are the slum areas of our larger cities and perhaps
some of the more remote and backward rural areas.  I propose that a
selection of such areas be made, and that the technique of interpene-
trating samples, as used by Mahalonobis and his colleagues in India,
be adapted for use here.  Briefly and imprecisely this technique calls
for the simultaneous administration of two independent censuses or
samples in the same area and at roughly the same time.  Knowing the
number enumerated in both censuses, the number enumerated in one but
not in the other, and vice versa, it is possible to make some estimate
of the number enumerated in neither.

A number of other such techniques are possible and might also
be explored in connection with the 1970 Census.  The Census Bureau has
conducted many experiments in connection with its annual or occasional
sample surveys but has been less willing to conduct large-scale experiments in connection with the decennial census.  This, however, is the
time when experiments could be most effectively performed, given the
necessary financial and human resources.

I would venture to say that every suggestion I have made has at some time been considered by the Census Bureau, and a number of them have been abandoned with reluctance. This year, as in all years, the Census Bureau is subject to great pressure to keep costs down, and by and large costs are kept down by maintaining an overlong interval between censuses, by simplifying the data collection techniques, and by holding down the number of items on the schedule; at a later stage the number of tabulations is limited and publications reduced. Curiously, the inventory of human resources in this country has seldom assumed the urgency that has been attached to counts of farms or businesses. The American public as a whole, and particularly the disadvantaged, would be greatly benefited if the handful of advocates of better population data in the Congress were joined by others.

However, more money will not in itself greatly improve the situation. Traditional census procedures, while highly effective, cannot be expected to provide the additional or better data needed in our effort to deal with the numerous problems posed by the disadvantaged. The Census Bureau has gone about as far as it can go with traditional procedures. Drastic changes are in order, some of them along the lines I have indicated. As much as possible should be done in 1970, but it is none too early to begin the planning for the quinquennial census of 1975.

VITAL STATISTICS FOR THE NEGRO, PUERTO RICAN,
AND MEXICAN POPULATIONS:  PRESENT QUALITY
AND PLANS FOR IMPROVEMENT

Robert D. Grove
Director, Division of Vital Statistics
National Center for Health Statistics

Evaluation of the quality of vital statistics for minority groups
in the United States should take into account (a) the quality of the
statistics for the majority group (white), and (b) the magnitude of the
between-group differences that are evidenced by reported statistics and
the degree to which they could be affected by incomplete reporting or
inaccurate classification.

## Completeness of Reporting

Information concerning the overall quality of national vital statistics is incomplete.  It can be said that adequate measures are
available for births and, perhaps, marriages.  Nation-wide tests of
birth registration completeness were made in conjunction with the population censuses of 1940 and 1950.  Current estimates are based on relationships established in those tests.  In 1965, the estimated degree
of completeness of the reported birth statistics for the United States
was 98.9 percent (white:  99.3 percent; nonwhite:  96.9 percent).

Similar quantitative measures of completeness of death registration are not available. It has proved very difficult to develop a technically acceptable method of checking death registration that is also feasible in cost terms. Several decades ago it was generally believed that death registration was more complete than birth registration. But today it is felt that, for the nation as a whole, birth and death registration are now about equally complete. There is evidence that infant deaths have been less completely registered than deaths at older ages. On the basis of a statistical analysis by Dr. Thomas N. E. Greville in connection with development of the methodology of the 1939-1941 decennial life tables, it has been assumed that infant death registration over the years has paralleled birth registration. This is obviously a convenient assumption because, if true, it means that the published infant mortality rates are correct.

Quantitative information is not available on the completeness of fetal death reporting for the entire country. Studies that have been made in certain cities and in connection with prepaid group medical care systems suggest that reporting of fetal deaths of twenty or more weeks gestation may be 65 to 75 percent complete for the total United States. Estimates of white-nonwhite differences have not been made. Another problem affecting the quality of national fetal death statistics is the variation among states in the legal requirements for reporting these events. The variation relates chiefly to the minimum gestational age to be reported.

The quality of marriage and divorce statistics is deficient in several ways. Following the historical precedents of the Birth and Death Registration Areas which were started early in this century to promote national statistics for these subjects, Marriage and Divorce Registration Areas were established by the Public Health Service in 1957 and 1958, respectively. At the present time there are twelve states which have not qualified for admission to the Marriage Registration Area and twenty-eight states are still outside the Divorce Registration Area.

Tests of completeness of marriage reporting have been conducted in eleven states and of divorce reporting in three states. In all areas the tests indicated that reporting was over 95 percent complete. We believe that this figure is representative of the results that will be obtained in other states in the Registration Areas. However, there are other deficiencies in the national statistics on these subjects. The marriage certificates of California, New Jersey, and Ohio do not ask for information on color or race. New York State will remove the question in 1968. One state (Ohio) does not include a question on race or color on its divorce record. In addition, the information is reported in only 62 percent of the records of the other states in the Divorce Registration Area which do ask the question. Also, information on race and other demographic characteristics, including age, is not available for inclusion in national statistics for states not in the Marriage and Divorce Registration Areas.

All states include a question on race or color on their birth, death, and fetal death certificate forms. Less than one percent of the records are arbitrarily classified due to omission of the information. In a number of states bills have been introduced in the legislature to remove questions on race from the various vital record

forms. However, except as we have already indicated for marriage
and divorce certificates, no state currently omits the question from
its records. One state health department did remove the question
from all of its forms several years ago but restored it within a
year.


## Accuracy of Reported Information

So far, we have considered the geographic coverage of national
vital statistics, completeness of reporting of vital events, and completeness of reporting of race information in these records. There
remains the question of accuracy of the reported information.

Most of our quantitative knowledge of accuracy is in the form
of consistency with the information in the population census and is
based on studies involving matched census and vital records for the
same individuals. It should be noted that this type of study cannot
verify the absolute accuracy of the data from either source, only the
agreement between information from the two sources. However, the degree of agreement between census and vital records is clearly important because they are used together to compute birth, death, marriage,
and divorce rates.

The nation-wide test of birth registration completeness in 1950
was mentioned previously. This test involved matching birth records
with census records of children enumerated in the census. The set of
matched records was used to measure the agreement of corresponding information given in the records as well as to determine completeness
of birth registration and census enumeration of infants. The follow-

ing pertinent results emerged: of those giving race as "white" on the birth certificate, 99.5 percent were also so identified in the census; for Negroes, the corresponding percentage of agreement was 98.7. Stated another way, the number of Negroes as counted from the birth records was 15/100ths of one percent larger than the number counted from the census records. This difference is not significant in relation to the differences in birth and fertility rates cited later. For whites and nonwhites, the reported age of mother on the two records agreed closely. Ninety-five percent of the white mothers and 90 percent of the nonwhite mothers were in the same five-year age interval in both records. In general, the discrepancies would not affect the comparative age-specific birth rates by race. Similar comparisons for Mexicans and Puerto Ricans are not available.

A large sample of certificates of deaths that occurred in the period, May-August 1960, was matched to records of the same persons listed in the population census taken as of April 1, 1960. The net differences in the racial designations on the two records were relatively small: 0.8 percent for whites and 1.1 percent for Negroes. They are not large enough to cast doubt on the validity of the interracial differences in mortality rates cited later. These figures can be compared to the net differences for Indians and Filipinos: 10 and 30 percent, respectively.

Differences between the vital and census records on reported age were also studied for the two broad groups, white and nonwhite. The comparison is given here for ten-year age groups by sex, beginning with the group 1-14 years. The results are shown in Table 1.

Figures preceded by a minus sign (-) indicate the percentage by which the census count exceeds the death record count in the table cell. It indicates that if the counts were adjusted to agree with each other the reported death rates would be increased. Figures not preceded by a minus sign indicate the percentage by which the death record count exceeds the census count. This indicates that if the counts were adjusted, the reported death rates would be reduced. These adjustments involve no assumption as to which count is correct, only the effects of making them agree.

The magnitude of the adjustments indicated by the matched record table can be compared with the differences between the reported and adjusted death rates, as shown in Table 2.

The excess nonwhite mortality at most ages, shown by the regularly published statistics, is confirmed by the rates adjusted for census-death certificate discrepancies in age reporting for all ages below 75. However, for males, aged 75-84, the higher rate for white males shown by usually published data disappears when the rates are adjusted for reporting discrepancies, and the rates for white and non-white males are identical when adjusted rates are used. For females, at ages 75-84, the reported excess for whites is replaced by an excess for nonwhites when the rates are adjusted. At ages 85 and over, for both males and females, the reported excess mortality for whites continues but is much reduced when the adjusted rates are compared.

Death rates for major causes of death have also been adjusted for discrepancies in age reporting. The excess nonwhite mortality reported for most causes is not changed when the adjusted rates are compared. Nonwhite male and female death rates for the cardiovascular diseases, cancer, accidents, influenza and pneumonia, diabetes, cirrhosis of the liver, and tuberculosis are substantially higher than the corresponding rates for the white population.

It would be desirable in assessing the accuracy of age-specific death rates to take account also of estimates of net undercount in the census and net underregistration by age. However, all of these data are not available. It should be noted also that comparisons of census and registration information do not provide a measure of accuracy of either source, only their degree of agreement. Independent measures of the accuracy of the two sets of data would be needed to determine the true rates. These measures are presently unavailable.

## Vital Rate Differences between Race Groups

From the viewpoint of analysis or policy determination, the significance of incomplete or inaccurate data is determined by the magnitude of the intergroup differences indicated by the reported statistics. The following data indicate very large differences between the mortality and fertility experiences of racial groups.

Table 3 gives comparative mortality and natality rates for the white, total nonwhite, and, when available, Negro groups in the United States in 1965. The differences are much larger than any known differences in the completeness of reporting events or the accuracy of reported information.

It will be observed that national data for Mexicans and Puerto Ricans are not included in the table. They are not available from regular national vital statistics tabulations or from the state offices. The reasons will be discussed later. However, data for persons born in Puerto Rico and resident in New York City were obtained through the courtesy of Louis Weiner, Director of the Bureau of Records and Statistics of the New York City Health Department. They are included in Table 4, which gives selected vital statistics for New York City.

Except for the age-adjusted death rate, the mortality rates for persons born in Puerto Rico are between those for the white and nonwhite populations. However, their birth and fertility rates are substantially higher than those of the other groups. It should be noted that data for Puerto Ricans include only those born in Puerto Rico because of the difficulty of defining others of Puerto Rican ancestry.

Vital statistics are not tabulated separately for Mexicans by the National Center for Health Statistics. Inquiries made to the two states with the largest Mexican populations, California and Texas, disclosed that such data have not been tabulated by their vital statistics offices. In an effort to obtain some information for this group, it was decided to compare the infant mortality rates for counties in five southwestern states in which, according to the 1960 census, 50 percent or more of the white population were persons of Spanish surname, with the rates for the total and total white populations of those states. Table 5 presents the results.

Infant deaths were not tabulated by color for most of the selected counties. However, it can be seen that there were relatively few nonwhite births so that the total infant mortality rate for those counties would be close to the rate for whites.

There is an indication that in the states of Arizona, Colorado, and New Mexico, counties with high proportions of Mexicans have higher rates of infant mortality than the total or the white population of the entire states. In Texas, the rates are about the same. These data are, of course, unsatisfactory. We should like to compare directly the rates for the Mexican, other white, and nonwhite populations. The following data are taken from a special tabulation of deaths among the foreign-born populations of the United States in the three-year period, 1959-1961. The table compares the age-adjusted death rates per 100,000 population for persons born in Mexico with rates for the total white and nonwhite populations in the United States:

|                | Total   | Male    | Female |
|----------------|---------|---------|--------|
| White          | 718.8   | 906.3   | 549.7  |
| Nonwhite       | 1,026.1 | 1,185.4 | 878.5  |
| Born in Mexico | 769.6   | 872.4   | 659.0  |

Data from the matched death-census record study mentioned earlier indicate a 1.9 percent difference between the two sources with respect to identification of persons born in Mexico. This discrepancy does not significantly affect the death rate differences shown.

Summary

The problem posed by the title of this paper, the quality of vital statistics for Negroes, Mexicans, and Puerto Ricans, can be solved only if there are adequate data specific for these population groups and objective measures of their accuracy. It can be inferred from the statistics cited in this paper that data which completely satisfy these requirements are not available. The deficiencies can now be considered.

1. Most vital statistics tabulations by race or color show only the two broad groups, white and nonwhite. This is due to two principal factors, which may be interrelated. First, the numerical size of the non-Negro nonwhite groups is relatively small so that detailed cross-tabulations of data, for example, cause of death by age and sex, or age of mother by birth order, would result in many table cells with very small frequencies. Second, population data needed for computation of vital rates are available only for the broader white and nonwhite groupings in intercensal years.

2. Omission of separate statistics for Negroes is also partly due to the lack, until recently, of population estimates for them. However, since Negroes constitute a high proportion of the total nonwhite population (92 percent in 1960; and 92 percent of births and 95 percent of deaths in 1964) rates for the total nonwhite population approximate the rates for Negroes as indicated by the United States data in Table 3.

3. National vital statistics for Mexicans and Puerto Ricans are not available. Persons stated on the vital records to be Mexican or Puerto Rican have for several decades been classified and included with the white population in national vital statistics. Some data

for these groups are produced by local areas, for example, for persons born in Puerto Rico and resident in New York City.

Accurate identification of these groups for statistical purposes presents some difficulties. "Country of birth" would identify only persons born in Mexico or Puerto Rico and would not include those whose parents or grandparents were born in those countries. According to the 1960 census, only 15 percent of the persons with Spanish surnames and living in five southwestern states were born in Mexico. Only 69 percent of the Puerto Ricans enumerated in the 1960 census were born in Puerto Rico. Place of birth of parents is asked on the birth certificates but not on the death certificates of most states.

Another possibility would be to use the Spanish surname to identify these groups on vital records, as was done for Mexicans in the population censuses of 1950 and 1960. It would be necessary to use this information in conjunction with place of birth to identify more completely Mexicans and Puerto Ricans. In the five southwestern states for which the Spanish surname was coded in the 1960 census, the combined total of foreign-born white persons of Spanish surname and of persons born in Mexico was 566,300. Of these persons only 83 percent were both born in Mexico and of Spanish surname; 12 percent were of Spanish surname but not born in Mexico; and 6 percent were born in Mexico but did not have a Spanish surname. Although similar data are not available for the native born it is probable that they would show a similar pattern. Thus Spanish surname and place of birth together would not provide complete identification of Mexican Americans. The nativity distribution of persons of Spanish surname in the five states was as follows:

| | |
|---|---|
| Total | 100.0 percent |
|    Native born, native parentage | 54.8 percent |
|    Native born, foreign or mixed parentage | 29.7 percent |
|    Foreign born | 15.4 percent |

Since 55 percent were native born of native parents, and some would not have Spanish surnames, all Mexican Americans could not be identified.

There are three final points to be made on the possibility and feasibility of providing the missing data:

1. Assuming that the additional tabulating costs can be justified, it would be possible to tabulate all vital statistics for Negroes separately. To make these data fully useful by computation of rates, it would be necessary for the Bureau of the Census to continue to include the Negro category in its various postcensal population estimates.

2. Annual coding, tabulation, and publication of vital statistics by Spanish surname and country of birth would involve substantial additional coding costs. Again, it would be desirable to have corresponding postcensal population estimates so that birth and death rates could be computed.

3. It must be noted that all vital statistics for minority groups are threatened by efforts to remove questions on race from

birth, death, and marriage records. During recent years bills have
been introduced in several state legislatures to eliminate race information from all vital records. None have so far been enacted into
law, although a few states have by law removed the question from the
marriage record.

Table 1.   PERCENTAGE DIFFERENCE BETWEEN DEATH CERTIFICATES
AND CENSUS TOTALS, 1960

| Age Group | Male | | Female | |
| --- | --- | --- | --- | --- |
| | White | Nonwhite | White | Nonwhite |
| 1–14 | – 0.6 | – 1.3 | – 0.9 | – 1.7 |
| 5–14 | 0.2 | 0.4 | – 1.5 | – 2.3 |
| 15–24 | 0.2 | – 2.9 | – 1.8 | – 4.8 |
| 25–34 | – 4.0 | – 3.2 | – 4.9 | – 2.4 |
| 35–44 | – 4.1 | – 1.9 | – 4.0 | – 1.1 |
| 45–54 | – 1.2 | 6.2 | – 1.3 | 13.3 |
| 55–64 | 0.2 | 13.6 | – 0.6 | 23.6 |
| 65–74 | – 0.3 | 2.1 | – 2.8 | – 4.5 |
| 75–84 | 1.2 | –15.1 | 2.5 | –17.2 |
| 85–99 | 1.9 | –23.3 | 2.8 | –21.5 |

(–)   Census total higher.

Table 2.  PUBLISHED AND ADJUSTED AGE-SPECIFIC DEATH RATES PER 1,000
POPULATION, BY SEX, COLOR, AND TEN-YEAR AGE INTERVALS,
UNITED STATES, 1960

| Age | Males | | | Females | | |
|---|---|---|---|---|---|---|
| | Pub-lished | Ad-justed | Percent-age Dif-ference | Pub-lished | Ad-justed | Percent-age Dif-ference |
| WHITE | | | | | | |
| 1-4 years | 1.0 | 1.0 | - 1.0 | 0.9 | 0.9 | - 2.7 |
| 5-14 | 0.5 | 0.5 | 1.4 | 0.3 | 0.3 | - 3.9 |
| 15-24 | 1.4 | 1.4 | - 1.1 | 0.5 | 0.5 | - 4.2 |
| 25-34 | 1.6 | 1.7 | - 3.3 | 0.9 | 1.1 | -14.9 |
| 35-44 | 3.3 | 3.5 | - 6.0 | 1.9 | 2.0 | - 7.0 |
| 45-54 | 9.3 | 9.4 | - 1.1 | 4.6 | 4.6 | - 0.9 |
| 55-64 | 22.3 | 22.5 | - 1.1 | 10.8 | 11.0 | - 2.0 |
| 65-74 | 48.5 | 48.0 | 1.1 | 27.8 | 28.3 | - 1.8 |
| 75-84 | 103.0 | 102.4 | 0.6 | 77.0 | 74.1 | 3.9 |
| 85 years and over | 217.5 | 211.2 | 3.0 | 194.8 | 190.2 | 2.4 |
| NONWHITE | | | | | | |
| 1-4 years | 2.1 | 2.2 | - 2.4 | 1.7 | 1.7 | -- |
| 5-14 | 0.8 | 0.8 | - 2.9 | 0.5 | 0.5 | - 4.1 |
| 15-24 | 2.1 | 2.1 | - 1.2 | 1.1 | 1.2 | -11.0 |
| 25-34 | 3.9 | 4.1 | - 5.6 | 2.6 | 2.8 | - 8.2 |
| 35-44 | 7.3 | 7.7 | - 4.7 | 5.5 | 5.4 | 2.1 |
| 45-54 | 15.5 | 14.5 | 7.2 | 11.4 | 9.7 | 18.1 |
| 55-64 | 31.5 | 27.5 | 14.4 | 24.1 | 19.4 | 24.2 |
| 65-74 | 56.6 | 56.4 | 0.3 | 39.8 | 43.0 | - 7.5 |
| 75-84 | 86.6 | 102.4 | -15.4 | 67.1 | 78.9 | -15.0 |
| 85 years and over | 152.4 | 179.7 | -15.2 | 128.7 | 179.7 | -28.4 |

A negative percentage difference means that the adjusted rate is
larger than the published rate.

Table 3. COMPARATIVE MORTALITY AND NATALITY RATES FOR WHITE, TOTAL NONWHITE, AND NEGRO POPULATION IN THE UNITED STATES, 1965

|  | White | Total Nonwhite | Negro |
|---|---|---|---|
| Age-adjusted death rate per 1,000 population | 7.1 | 10.3 | -- |
| Expectation of life at birth (years) | 71.0 | 64.1 | -- |
| Infant mortality rate (per 1,000 live births) | 21.5 | 40.3 | 41.7 |
| Maternal mortality rate (per 100,000 live births) | 21.0 | 83.7 | 88.3 |
| Birth rate (per 1,000 population) | 18.3 | 27.6 | -- |
| General fertility rate (per 1,000 women, 15-44 years) | 91.4 | 133.9 | -- |
| Rate of fifth and higher order births (per 1,000 women, 15-44 years) | 13.1 | 37.1 | -- |
| Illegitimate birth ratio (per 1,000 live births) | 39.6 | 263.2 | -- |
| Percentage of births occurring in hospitals | 98.9 | 89.8 | -- |
| Percentage of births not attended by physician | 0.5 | 8.2 | -- |

Table 4.   SELECTED VITAL STATISTICS FOR NEW YORK CITY, 1959–1961

|  | White | Nonwhite (chiefly Negro) | Born in Puerto Rico |
|---|---|---|---|
| Age-adjusted death rate (5 years and over, per 1,000 population) | | | |
| Male | 13.1 | 16.0 | 10.0 |
| Female | 9.3 | 11.6 | 8.2 |
| Infant mortality rate (per 1,000 live births) | 20.1 | 41.7 | 30.2 |
| Maternal mortality rate (per 1,000 live births) | 3.1[*] | 12.5[*] | 9.8[*] |
| Birth rate (per 1,000 population) | 17.5 | 31.0 | 55.8 |
| General fertility rate (per 1,000 women, 15–44 years) | 90.5 | 121.5 | 165.5 |

[*]Data for 1965.

- 116 -

Table 5.  INFANT MORTALITY RATES FOR COUNTIES IN WHICH 50 PERCENT OR
MORE OF WHITE POPULATION IN 1960 WERE PERSONS OF SPANISH
SURNAME AND FOR SELECTED STATES, 1965

| | Live Births | | Deaths Under 1 Year | | | |
|---|---|---|---|---|---|---|
| | Total | White | Total | Rate per 1,000 Live Births | White | Rate per 1,000 Live Births |
| Arizona | | | | | | |
| Entire state | 33,922 | 27,964 | 861 | 25.4 | 605 | 21.6 |
| 2 counties | 494 | 488 | 13 | 26.3 | -- | -- |
| California | | | | | | |
| (0 counties) | | | | | | |
| Colorado | | | | | | |
| Entire state | 36,784 | 34,900 | 895 | 24.3 | 837 | 24.0 |
| 3 counties | 408 | 406 | 16 | 39.2 | -- | -- |
| New Mexico | | | | | | |
| Entire state | 24,310 | 20,918 | 655 | 26.9 | 535 | 25.6 |
| 8 counties | 4,122 | 3,668 | 129 | 31.3 | -- | -- |
| Texas | | | | | | |
| Entire state | 215,708 | 180,506 | 5,608 | 26.0 | 4,161 | 23.1 |
| 16 counties | 17,936 | 17,896 | 460 | 25.6 | -- | -- |

NEEDED STATISTICS FOR MINORITY GROUPS
IN METROPOLITAN AREAS

Daniel O. Price
Department of Sociology
University of Texas

We get a snapshot of the population when the census is taken.
There are shortcomings and difficulties to this which are discussed
in other papers in this collection. However, from present census
data we do not get much indication of change for individuals and
families. It is important to know where a person is, but it is
equally important, and in some cases more important, to know in
which direction a person is moving. For example, we may know that
two individuals each received $5,000 in income during the previous
twelve months. They are at the same point in income. However, if
five years ago one of them earned $3,000 and the other earned
$10,000, then we have important additional information about them.
One of them is apparently on his way up and the other is losing
ground.

In my opinion the main additional data that we need for the
population of the United States, and which are especially relevant
for minority groups in urban areas, are data on social mobility.

Beginning in 1940 the census began collecting data on geographic mobility by asking a question on place of residence five

years previously. (Questions on the state of birth had provided some information of this sort for many decades.) It is not possible, of course, to ask the question, "Where were you in the social structure five years ago?" (I am sure such a question would yield some interesting answers, but I doubt if they could be tabulated.) How then do we go about getting information on social mobility?

Unfortunately, social mobility is far more complex than geographic mobility, and further research and development work needs to be done on its measurement. When we realize that the goals of the poverty program, welfare programs, educational programs, and many others, are to produce some sort of social mobility, it is surprising that so little attention has been given to its measurement. There are other ways of attempting to evaluate the consequences of these government programs that account for such large expenditures of tax money, but a more direct measurement of progress, measurement of upward movement or lack of upward movement, should be undertaken.

There are dangers, of course, in attempting to measure social mobility, especially as social mobility might be a consequence of efforts made by government programs. Because of ease of measurement, there may be acceptance of too simple a measure. Some people would measure social change and the effectiveness of a program by asking simply whether or not it produced changes in earnings of the individuals involved. A change in earnings is a part of social mobility, but a change in attitudes, a change in political behavior, changes in patterns of expenditures, may all be important parts of social mobility.

I am not going to suggest that the census should collect atti-
tudinal data, but it is important to realize that the aspects of social
change that we can measure most easily do not constitute complete measures of social change. And just because a program does not produce
immediate changes in measurable variables this should not be taken to
indicate that the program is ineffective. "Great Society" is doubtless within our reach, but "Instant Great Society" certainly is not.

One of the pieces of information that can be collected more
easily and that would give insights into change in status and position
of individuals is the social security number. We are all aware of the
opposition to inclusion of this in the census data because of the fear
of misuse. I insist that it is possible to establish and implement
adequate safeguards against misuse of computer stored data. By turning check writing procedures over to electronic data processing ma-
chines, we have effectively stored millions of dollars in the ma-
chines; and the misuse of these funds is adequately safeguarded. An
unauthorized person is not permitted to make an expenditure from the
machine. Why could not analogous safeguards be set up to prevent unauthorized expenditure of data from a machine?

What sorts of things could we gain from having the social security number? There are two general areas in which it can provide
much additional information. The first of these advantages would come
only after the social security number had been collected for two successive censuses. When this occurs, it will then be possible to match
records from one census to the next and to have data on changes in all
of the characteristics on which the census collects data. In the

first place, this would add another dimension to information on geographic mobility. Assuming that the question on residence five years
earlier is continued, this would provide information on residence ten
years earlier, and then twenty years earlier, and so on.

Even more important than geographic mobility, however, would be
information on occupation ten years earlier. This would make it possible to look both at occupational changes and at the extent to which
occupational changes are associated with geographic mobility. Information on occupational changes is one of the most important aspects of
social mobility.

It would be possible to put together information on educational
changes. We generally assume that the level of education does not
change significantly after age twenty-five, but given record linkages
with social security numbers, it would be possible to examine changes
in education after age twenty-five and the extent to which these are
associated with changes in occupation.

Changes in income could be examined in relation to changes in
occupation and level of education. Are there income handicaps that
a person faces if he changes occupation at an older age? To what extent are there regular patterns of occupational change with increasing
age, and how are these changes related to income?

If young children had social security numbers, as may well be
the case in the not too distant future, it would be possible to examine educational progress during this ten-year period. For example,
what are the demographic characteristics of children who in ten years
of school do not advance ten years in grade? This is to ask, what are

the characteristics of children who become educationally retarded? What is the eventual education of children who are educationally retarded or educationally advanced in earlier years? These and many other studies would be possible if census records could be linked from one decade to the next.

Moreover, changes in marital status associated with changes in residence and occupation could be examined. At the present time we do not know how much migration is a consequence of change in marital status.

In addition to linking census records from one census to the next, it would be possible to link census data with information on individuals from other sources. One of the most fruitful linkages would doubtless be with information in the social security program itself. Here information on income and occupation changes would be available for combination with census characteristics. Linking changes in income and occupation over a ten-year period provides one sort of measure of social mobility, but changes from year to year provide additional important information. Changes in employment by company would also be available. A person may change from one company to another without any change in occupation or residence. The extent to which these sorts of change accompany or precede changes in income could be examined.

Information from social security and other sources could also be used for the purpose of examining the quality of information collected by the census. Record checks from independent sources of data provide one of the most feasible ways to evaluate the accuracy of census responses. The inaccuracy of other sources of data must also be considered, of course.

The collection of information on the social security number would thus open up much additional data on the changing characteristics of individuals through the linkage both with previous census records and with other records.

It has been suggested that the social security number be collected on a 25 percent sample. If this is done, then a maximum of one in sixteen individuals could have records linked from one census to another, and for less than one in sixty-four would it be possible to link records for a twenty-year period, assuming a social security number for each individual. If you are studying the characteristics of individuals who have changed marital status during this period, the sample may well be too small to be most useful, because it must be broken down by age, sex, color, and place of residence to begin with. There are many reasons why it is important to collect information on social security number on a 100 percent basis. A 25 percent basis would be better than nothing, but a 100 percent basis is desirable.

There are other sorts of questions that would provide information on social mobility, but no single question that would provide as much information. It would be possible, for example, to ask occupation one, two, or five years earlier in order to obtain information on occupational changes. This would provide more recent information on occupational changes than would be available from census record linkages but it would probably include large errors due to problems of recall. However, such a question should be asked if the social security number is not obtained.

Questions on fertility are being designed which would provide information on change--date of birth of last child, date of birth of first child, date of beginning of present marital status, date of first marriage if present marriage is not the first, and so on. These questions are important in order to provide additional information on changes in the characteristics of individuals or changes in the status of individuals. It is to be hoped that as many as possible of these questions will survive into the 1970 census. The present drops in the crude birth rate should not lull us into a feeling of security that population growth is no longer a problem. Population growth is still a major problem.

Additional snapshot or cross-sectional information is also needed. Some of the most important information of this sort is that which the Carnegie Corporation's Exploratory Committee on Assessing the Progress of Education, under the chairmanship of Ralph W. Tyler, proposes to collect: information on the quality of education as measured by tests and observations of population samples.[1] Much opposition has developed to such a program, even among many educators. However, it seems reasonable to evaluate at least some of the results of the public systems of education because such a large amount of tax money goes into them. The opposition stems in part from the dangers already cited about the measurement of the consequences of any program designed to produce social change. Those aspects of change that are

---

[1] See Ralph W. Tyler, "Assessing the Progress of Education," Pro-ceedings of the Social Statistics Section of the American Statistical Association (1966).

most easily measured may not be those that are most important, and it is almost certain that no test can adequately measure all of the effects of public education. There is fear that those consequences of public education that can be measured will be taken as the only standards of quality in educational systems. But just because only some of the effects of education can be measured we should not be deterred from measuring those that can be measured. The general public and public officials need to realize that such measurements are extremely useful but should not be taken as the sole criteria for evaluating an educational system.

Measurement of student achievement on a national basis, with the opportunity for area comparisons, would be extremely valuable. In many ways, such information on school systems would be analogous to information yielded by the National Teacher Examination. This potentially provides information on teacher preparation by colleges and universities. A nationally administered test of some aspects of the quality of education would provide important information on the training being offered in various school systems. (The Tyler Committee does not propose to collect information on school systems.) This would also provide information on the quality of education of individuals in relation to the skill level at which they are employed. A justification frequently cited for the quality of employment offered to Negroes is the quality of education which they have received. A national test of educational achievement would either indicate that the employment level was not at the educational achievement level for Negroes or it would provide important information on the necessity for further improvement in the quality of education offered to minority groups.  It might not be feasible to collect such information on educational achievement as part of a census program, but this in no way minimizes the importance of such information.

Another area that is important regards assistance from poverty or welfare programs.  It might be possible to collect such information by matching records through the social security numbers, but it is generally assumed that social security numbers are least accurate and least prevalent in this particular group.  Therefore it would be important to ask directly about the amount and type of assistance or training from welfare or poverty programs.  There is opposition to such a question because of the established position that the receipt of public assistance should not be public information.  No census information is available at the individual level, therefore there would be no violation of the confidential nature of such information.  With such data and with census information available at more frequent periods than at present, it would be possible to evaluate the effects of these programs.

One might argue that most of this information is already available in the files of the poverty program and welfare agencies.  Much of the information is certainly available for current recipients of welfare, but the files can never provide the important information regarding what happened to the recipient after he went off the rolls. A question of this sort on a census basis would be able to provide information on the current occupation, income, and so on, of individuals who were receiving assistance two, three, or five years before.  It seems that this is the information that is needed for a proper evaluation of these programs, to find out the sorts of individuals and households that are most helped and the sorts that seem to benefit very little.

With this question, as with any new question, research would be needed to determine how it might best be asked and to evaluate the quality of responses. This latter factor might provide a real problem.

It would be valuable for a proper understanding of the social dynamics of the population to have information on the aspirations and values of the people. However, I am not going to suggest that we try to measure achievement motivation and other values in a census type situation, even though the information would be extremely useful. A simple question that seems to provide some information on this is the one on religious preference. Privately sponsored research that has collected information on religious preference has found that the classification of individuals by religious preference differentiates them on many characteristics and patterns of behavior.

The opposition to this question on grounds of the separation of church and state is well known, but experience indicates that less than one percent of the population objects to answering such a question.

If such information were available it might be possible to throw some light on the decline in the number of Negro ministers. The decline in many areas makes it appear that Negro males are losing ground badly in employment in the professional and technical occupations. If ministers are excluded from consideration, we frequently find gains in employment in the other professional and technical occupations or at least much smaller losses in relative employment. Information on religious preference might throw light on this phenomenon, but it would be more important in understanding differential patterns of behavior.

Other information that would be useful to have, and on which the Census Bureau is gaining some experience, I believe, relates to voting behavior. The census would not, of course, ask for whom a person voted but whether or not the individual was a registered voter and whether or not he voted in the most recent election, whenever it might have been. It would be interesting and useful to have information on some measure of political knowledge, but I doubt if it is feasible to suggest asking questions in this area.

There are many other topics on which it would be valuable to have data that could be related to the information available in the census. One of these would be data on the quality of housing. The use of a mail-out/mail-back census questionnaire means that for most structures there is no longer an interviewer on the site to evaluate the quality of the housing. These interviewer evaluations had fairly low reliability, and the Census Bureau has been working on alternative approaches to collect such information. It is important to know, if possible, something of the quality of the housing in relation to the characteristics of individuals and in relation to the rent paid.

It would also be useful if information on crime and delinquency were available, but I am sufficiently realistic to know that this would be impossible unless, for the purpose of research in this area, record linkages by social security number could be made.

In terms of individuals' adaptation to the urban environment, two other items of information would be useful. One of these relates to farm background and the other to the country or nationality of origin. It has been suggested that the question might be asked, "Did this person live on a farm or in a rural area at age sixteen?" This would certainly provide some information regarding a rural background or an early experience with urban living. For example, rural background seems to be closely related to fertility in urban areas, and it is almost certainly related to other patterns of behavior that affect adjustment to urban living.

The country or nationality of origin is important for a better evaluation of the social condition of minority groups, such as Puerto Ricans and Mexican Americans. The Census Bureau has been experimenting with ways of asking such a question and is bothered by the number of combinations that people report--such as Scotch-Irish. It is believed that further pretesting will result in a suitable question with structured alternatives, and it is hoped that such a question will be used in the 1970 census.

In this paper several suggestions have been made for additional questions, and it is not likely that all of these could be financially supported. However, it is most desirable that some question on social mobility should be included. This might be such a simple question as "What was this person doing five years ago?" with a check list of alternative responses: (1) at work, (2) in armed forces, (3) in school, (4) other. The addition of information on occupation and industry, for those at work, would increase the value tremendously. The five-year period is suggested so that this question might be related to the one on geographic residence five years previously.

The social security number is also important and should be included. This would not be a substitute for the question on activities five years previously but would provide important supplementary information. Potentially it could provide some of the answers to the question on activities five years previously; but it would provide biased coverage until a larger proportion of the population has a social security number.

Information on national background or country of origin is important if we are to assess areas of discrimination and social change. Information on quality of education should be collected, but there is some question as to whether or not it should be collected by the government at this time.

Data on the receipt of assistance from some poverty program or public welfare program would be most useful for a better evaluation of these programs. Information on rural background would help in understanding problems of adjustment to urban areas.

A recent government contract made available over $1 million to study people's reactions to airport noise. At approximately the same time a suggestion that the government should finance a $1 million study of farm labor problems was considered completely unreasonable. It is important that we recognize the major problems of American society and allocate our resources in an efficient manner. And the problems of minority groups in metropolitan areas certainly rank among the major problems of our society today.  If we are to deal with them

in an even partially satisfactory manner, adequate information must

be available.  As a move in this direction, it is hoped that financial

support can be made available for the collection of some of the infor-

mation suggested here.

APPENDIX


AN EVALUATION OF COVERAGE IN THE 1960 CENSUS OF POPULATION BY
TECHNIQUES OF DEMOGRAPHIC ANALYSIS AND BY COMPOSITE METHODS[*]


Jacob S. Siegel and Melvin Zelnik[†]
U. S. Bureau of the Census


## Method of Demographic Analysis

Introduction. This paper presents (1) the results of studies
using methods of demographic analysis to evaluate the 1960 Census
counts and (2) several sets of composite estimates which combine (a)
the results derived by various analytic techniques or (b) the results
derived by analytic techniques and the case-by-case checking techniques involving reinterviews and matching against independent lists,
which are discussed in a companion paper by Marks and Waksberg.[‡]  Because of the close relation between coverage of the total population
and the accuracy of the data by age, sex, and color, we are concerned
here both with overall underenumeration and with net undercounts (or
overcounts) by age, sex, and color.

---

[*]Reprinted from the 1966 Social Statistics Section Proceedings
of the American Statistical Association.

[†]Dr. Zelnik has been associated with the School of Hygiene and
Public Health, Johns Hopkins University, since August 1966.

The authors wish to make special acknowledgment of the contribution of Leon Pritzker of the U. S. Bureau of the Census in connection with the conceptual development of the composite estimates.

[‡]Eli S. Marks and Joseph Waksberg, "Evaluation of Coverage in
the 1960 Census of Population through Case-by-Case Checking," Proceedings of the Social Statistics Section, American Statistical Association
(1960), pp. 62-70.

There are a variety of specific techniques of evaluation that may be classified as techniques of demographic analysis. These techniques make possible the comparison of census counts with some expected result or standard usually derived by the manipulation of such demographic data as census counts and birth, death, and immigration data. There are a number of limitations to these techniques. First, the expected results or standards may be defective, either because of errors in the data underlying them or because of oversimplified assumptions in their construction. Second, these techniques serve best to provide estimates of census error which are relative to a previous census or to other categories in the same census rather than absolute estimates of error. Third, these techniques provide measures of net census error only, that is, they cannot distinguish between content and coverage error or between compensating overcoverage and undercoverage. Thus, for example, in dealing with the population of the United States classified by age, sex, and color, the method cannot distinguish between coverage error and errors in classifying persons by age, sex, and color.

The advantages of these techniques are, basically, that they deal with an entire universe or subuniverse and are, for the most part, not handicapped by sampling error or the problems of matching; they focus on levels of error which may be more effectively measured, for example, net census error or deviations from expected ratios; and the defects of the standards or expected results may be small. In addition, the techniques of demographic analysis often provide a strong basis for judging the demographic reasonableness of census results and of other methods of evaluation.

Although the analytic techniques cannot identify the sources of error, it is still advisable to maintain a conceptual distinction vis-à-vis these sources. Thus, when the focus of our analysis is on the total population, the estimated net errors are estimates of coverage error only. In this context we shall use the term "net under-enumeration." When the focus of the analysis is on some segment of the total population, for example, a specific age-sex-color group, the net error actually refers to the joint effect of both errors of coverage and errors of classification. In this context, we shall use the term "net undercount (or overcount)."

Intercensal Estimating Equation. An estimate of the accuracy of the 1960 Census count relative to the 1950 Census count can be arrived at by comparing the difference between the two census figures, on the one hand, and the algebraic sum of the estimates of the components of change during the decade, on the other. If the former figure is larger than the latter figure, then the absolute amount of net census under-enumeration has decreased; if the latter is larger, then the absolute amount of net census underenumeration has increased. This assumes that the estimate of net change based on components is without error. Several reports and papers have presented the results of comparisons of this kind.[1] The latest Census Bureau's report giving intercensal popu-

---

[1]See U. S. Bureau of the Census, Current Population Reports, Series P-25, Nos. 331 and 310; Donald S. Akers, "Estimating Net Census Undercount in 1960 Using Analytical Techniques," paper presented at the annual meeting of the Population Association of America, Madison, Wisconsin, May 1962; and Conrad Taeuber and Morris H. Hansen, "A

lation estimates for 1950 to 1960 implies that the amount of net underenumeration was almost exactly the same (difference of 3,000) in 1960
as in 1950. However, in their study published in Demography, Taeuber
and Hansen gave an estimate of an increase in coverage of 277,000 between 1950 and 1960. The difference in these two estimates is a result
of different assumptions concerning the amount of net migration of
U. S. citizens (exclusive of those moving between Puerto Rico and the
United States).[2]

Taeuber and Hansen note another element of uncertainty in the
determination of the relative levels of coverage in the two censuses,
namely, the possibility of overenumeration in the 1960 Census figures
due to overimputation of persons. The authors state that the range
of this overenumeration could reasonably be from 100,000 to 400,000.
However, they do not make an allowance for overimputation in their
estimates.

If we make maximum and minimum allowances for overimputation
and net movement of U. S. citizens, we can generate a range of estimates for the change in coverage between 1950 and 1960. Thus, assuming 400,000 overimputations and a net in-migration of 280,000 U. S.
citizens, we have a reduced coverage of 403,000 in 1960. Alternatively, assuming no overimputations and a net out-migration of 172,000
U. S. citizens, we have an increased coverage of 449,000 in 1960.

---

Preliminary Evaluation of the 1960 Censuses of Population and Housing,"
Demography, Vol. I, No. 1 (1964).

[2] On the basis of the two available estimates of net movement of
this group (-172,000 and +280,000), Taeuber and Hansen assumed zero net
movement while the other studies had adopted the figure of +280,000.

Table 1 shows, for various estimates of the percentage net underenumeration in 1950, the percentage of net underenumeration in 1960 assuming the following changes in absolute coverage between 1950 and 1960: (a) no change; (b) an increase of 277,000; (c) a decrease of 403,000; and (d) an increase of 449,000. If the net underenumeration in 1950 was 1.4 percent, as indicated by the 1950 Post-Enumeration Survey, and if the absolute decrease in coverage between 1950 and 1960 was 403,000, then the percentage net underenumeration was the same in 1960 as in 1950. All other comparisons show a smaller percentage underenumeration in 1960 than in 1950.

Estimates by Age, Sex, and Color. Estimates have also been obtained of the relative consistency of the 1950 and 1960 Census counts by age, sex, and color. The residuals derived by comparing the expected population in 1960, based on the 1950 Census counts and data on births, deaths, and net immigration, with the census counts in 1960 also represent the differences between the net undercounts in 1960 and 1950 for age cohorts, assuming that the estimates of intercensal change based on component data are without error. The estimates of intercensal change used to bring the 1950 Census figures forward are consistent with an overall estimate of no change (3,000) in absolute coverage between 1950 and 1960. The estimates of intercensal change and the resulting residual estimates have been set forth in Current Population Reports, Series P-25, No. 310.[3] Such estimates are

---

[3] U. S. Bureau of the Census, "Estimates of the Population of the United States and Components of Change, by Age, Color, and Sex, 1950 to 1960," Current Population Reports, Series P-25, No. 310, by J. S. Siegel, D. S. Akers, and W. D. Jones (June 30, 1965).

of quite limited usefulness, however, in establishing the net undercounts in the later census, since it is almost impossible to eliminate
from the residuals the contribution of errors in the earlier census.
They may, however, direct attention to possible anomalies in one or
the other census, for example, the apparently large net overcount of
persons 65 and over in 1960, especially of nonwhites (13 percent for
each sex), an anomaly which has now appeared in three successive censuses.

Some analytic studies carried out at the Census Bureau have
yielded estimates of absolute coverage of population by age, sex, and
color in 1960. In Current Population Reports, Series P-25, No. 310,
adjusted census data for 1950 and 1960 were employed in preparing intercensal estimates of the population from 1950 to 1960. The adjustments in 1960 were derived by carrying adjusted census figures for
1950 forward to 1960 by estimates of intercensal change and then comparing the results with the 1960 Census counts. In the case of whites,
the estimates of net census undercounts for 1950 for ages 15 and over
were those developed by Coale and Zelnik for native whites.[4]

The Coale-Zelnik estimates of net undercounts for native whites
aged 15 and over are based on estimates of births for 1855-1934, which
in turn result from the backward projection of females aged 15-29 in

---

[4]Ansley J. Coale and Melvin Zelnik, New Estimates of Fertility
and Population in the United States (Princeton, N. J.: Princeton University Press, 1963). Other estimates of net undercounts for (native)
whites in 1960 than those described in the text are shown in M. Zelnik, "Errors in the 1960 Census Enumeration of Native Whites," Journal
of the American Statistical Association, Vol. 59 (June 1964), pp. 437-
459.

the eight censuses from 1880 to 1950 and the assumption of a uniform level of net undercount of these females amounting to 1.4 percent. Coale and Zelnik found that the figures for white female births obtained by "reviving" native white females enumerated in the age span 15-29 were consistently higher than comparable estimates of the same birth cohorts derived by "reviving" females enumerated for ages below 15 and above 30; that is, females aged 15-29 appeared to be the most fully enumerated group. The estimate of 1.4 percent is offered as the minimum net undercount implied by the available evidence and is associated in part with a net undercount of 1.0 percent for white women 15-54 years of age as shown by the 1950 Post-Enumeration Survey. The assumption of a net undercount of females aged 15-29 in recent censuses, combined with the fact that births estimated from females aged 15-29 in one census are (approximately) equal to births estimated from females aged 15-29 in the preceding and following censuses, led to the assumption of uniform net undercounts over time. In order to derive estimates of male births, female births were inflated by a constant sex ratio at birth; this was equivalent to increasing births estimated from males by 3 percent, on the average.

The estimates of net undercounts for nonwhites 15 years old and over in 1950 were derived by a variation of Coale's iterative technique, using an assumption that the percentage of net undercount in 1940 for each 5-year age group below age 35 and each 10-year age group 35 and over was the same as the average of the percentages of net undercount for the same age groups in 1950 and 1960.[5] In the case of

_____

[5]The results were adjusted by the application of sex ratios

- 138 -

both whites and nonwhites, estimates of net undercounts under 15 years of age in 1950 were determined by use of birth statistics adjusted for underregistration, brought forward with allowance for changes due to death and migration. Tables 2 (col. 2) and 3 (col. 4) give the resulting percentage of net undercounts by age, sex, and color, for the resident population of the United States in 1960.[6]

Recent work suggests that the pattern of net undercounts by age in 1960 is markedly different from the patterns in 1950, 1940, and 1930, even though the age patterns in the three earlier censuses are not too dissimilar one from another.[7] As a result of this difference, the iterative technique linking 1950 and 1960 is probably not a suitable technique for estimating net undercounts in 1960, as was done for the nonwhite estimates in Series P-25, No. 310. We have, therefore, prepared alternative estimates of net undercounts in 1960 for the nonwhite population carrying forward the original Coale estimates of adjusted nonwhite population in 1950 (that is, those published in 1955)

_____

based on quasi-generation life tables. The estimates for 10-year groups in 1950 were then distributed into 5-year groups by a graduation method. See, also, Akers, op. cit.

[6]The estimates of intercensal change used to bring the 1950 adjusted census figures forward are consistent with an estimate of no change (3,000) in overall coverage between 1950 and 1960; the figures are those shown in Table 12 of Current Population Reports, Series P-25, No. 310. The estimates of net undercounts in 1960, shown in Tables C-2 of that report, refer to the total population of conterminous United States (excluding Alaska and Hawaii), including members of the Armed Forces overseas, and are based on the population adjusted for net undercounts.

[7]Melvin Zelnik, "An Examination of Alternative Estimates of Net Census Undercount, by Age, Sex, and Color: 1950 and 1960," paper contributed to the annual meeting of the Population Association of America, New York, N.Y., April 1966.

with our estimates of intercensal changes.[8]  The Coale estimates of

1950 were derived by an iterative technique on the general hypothe-

sis that the age patterns of net undercounts were similar in the 1930,

1940, and 1950 censuses, and on the specific conservative hypothesis

that the percentage errors in 1930 were equal to those of 1940 or

1950, whichever was less.  The least reliable results of this method

are at the older ages.  Accordingly, the Post-Enumeration Survey re-

sults were substituted for persons aged 65 and over.  The 1950 Coale

estimates extended to 1960 are offered here as no less reasonable

than, and possibly superior to, the other estimates available (see

Table 3, col. 5).

Estimates Based on Adjusted Births.  In all of the estimates

that have been presented up to this point, the expected populations

under age 15 in 1950 and under age 25 in 1960 are based on registered

births adjusted for underregistration, registered deaths, and esti-

mates of net migration.   Since the number of births in any period of

time is considerably larger than the number of deaths and net migrants,

errors in the completeness of birth registration are of greater con-

sequence for estimates of net census underenumeration and net census

undercounts than errors in the other components.

Two tests of the completeness of registration of births have

been conducted--one in conjunction with the 1940 Census, the other in

---

[8]A. J. Coale, "The Population of the United States in 1950 Classified by Age, Sex, and Color--A Revision of Census Figures," Journal
of the American Statistical Association, Vol. 50 (March 1955), pp. 16-
54; M. Zelnik, "An Examination of Alternative Estimates . . . ," op.
cit.

conjunction with the 1950 Census. The percentage completeness by color and occurrence in hospitals, according to these tests, is as follows:

| Year and Color | Total | In Hospital | Not in Hospital |
|---|---|---|---|
| 1940 | | | |
| All classes | 92.5 | 98.5 | 86.1 |
| White | 94.0 | 98.6 | 88.2 |
| Nonwhite | 82.0 | 96.3 | 77.2 |
| 1950 | | | |
| All classes | 97.9 | 99.4 | 88.2 |
| White | 98.6 | 99.5 | 88.2 |
| Nonwhite | 93.5 | 98.2 | 88.2 |

Estimates of the completeness of registration for the intercensal years 1940 to 1950 were derived by interpolating between the 1940 and 1950 test results. Specifically, it was assumed that the change in percentage completeness followed a linear trend between the decennial years with respect to hospital and nonhospital births, for the white and nonwhite groups separately, for each state.

No test of birth registration completeness was carried out in 1960. As a result, estimates of the completeness of birth registration for years subsequent to 1950 were based on the results of the 1950 test, on the assumption that percentage completeness by occurrence in hospital and not in hospital, by color and by state, was the same as in 1950. (In effect, an estimated change in registration for each color group comes about from changes in the proportion utilizing hospitals for childbirth.) Similarly, the results of the 1940 test were used to derive estimates of the completeness of birth registration for the years 1935-1939.

Although there were some differences in the designs of the two Birth Registration Tests, they consisted, essentially, of matching birth records that covered some specified period of time immediately preceding the census with cards prepared for infants born during that period and enumerated in the census. The major source of error in this procedure, ignoring problems of matching, involved infants who were not enumerated. If, among these persons, the proportion whose birth was not registered was the same as among those enumerated, then their omission from the census would not affect the estimate of completeness of birth registration. However, it is quite likely that among those not enumerated, the proportion whose birth was not registered was higher than among those enumerated. This would mean that estimates of the completeness of birth registration were too high, thereby introducing a downward bias in estimates of population based on adjusted births.

Chandra Sekar and Deming have examined the effect on the estimates of completeness of registration of the omission of infants in the census[9] and have suggested a method for estimating the bias. The basic objective of the method is to subdivide an area (either geographically or by a combination of characteristics) into subgroups each of which is highly homogeneous with respect to enumeration com-

---

[9]C. Chandra Sekar and W. E. Deming, "On a Method of Estimating Birth and Death Rates and the Extent of Registration," Journal of the American Statistical Association, Vol. 44, No. 245 (March 1949).

pleteness (a completely homogeneous population is defined as one in which each individual has an equal probability of being enumerated). Within such subgroups, the correlation between unregistered and un-enumerated events would be very low. An estimate of the total number of births (registered and unregistered) in the area could then be derived by cumulating the "total number of births" corrected for underregistration. Relating the figure for registered births to this total would then give a figure approximating the unbiased estimate of completeness of registration. This method was applied by the National Office of Vital Statistics to the results of the 1940 and 1950 tests-- in the former case to all states and in the latter to the state with the lowest registration completeness in 1950. The results indicated that underenumeration had little effect on estimates of registration completeness.

In a further attempt to explore this question, we have used the national results of the 1950 Birth Registration Test and the 1950 Infant Enumeration Study in conjunction with two assumptions of dependence between unregistered and unenumerated events to generate two alternative estimates of birth registration completeness in 1950 for the total United States. The assumptions we employed were that (a) the degree of "not registered" was zero for the "not enumerated" group, and (b) the degree of "not registered" for the "not enumerated" was ten times as great as the degree of "not registered" for the "enumerated." These two assumptions led to estimates of completeness of registration of 98.0 percent and 96.9 percent, respectively, as contrasted to the actual estimate of 97.9 percent. Thus, rather extreme assumptions had only very slight effects on the level of the completeness of registration.

Aside from the issue just discussed, it has been suggested that the results of the Birth Registration Tests are biased upward, especially in the case of nonwhites, because of the difficulties of establishing matches.[10] Since it is not possible at this date to examine the original documents, we have employed a fairly extreme assumption to measure the sensitivity of the estimates of net census undercount to an overestimate of the incompleteness of registration. We have assumed for illustrative purposes a reduction of one third in the annual estimates of the incompleteness of registration of births, by color. Table 4 compares the estimates of net census undercount, for the population under 25 years of age by age, sex, and color, based on the official estimates of the completeness of registration of births, with estimates employing the assumption stated. We want to emphasize that the results do not provide any information on the accuracy or inaccuracy of the official estimates of the completeness of birth registration. They merely indicate what the effect would be on estimates of net census undercount if the estimates of completeness of registration were in error by as large a margin as we have assumed. The effect is especially noticeable for nonwhites in the age groups 15–19 and 20–24. The estimate of net undercount of nonwhite males aged 20–24 is reduced from 21 to 11 percent; the corresponding figure for females is reduced from 11 percent to 2 percent.

_____

[10] D. J. Bogue, B. D. Misra, and D. P. Dandekar, "A New Estimate of the Negro Population and Negro Vital Rates in the United States, 1930–1960," Demography, Vol. I (1964).

We are inclined to accept the official estimates of completeness of birth registration, even though these estimates lead to large estimates of net census undercount for nonwhites, especially males. The estimates for nonwhite males aged 20-24 in 1960 arrived at through the use of the birth registration figures are not very different from the undercounts estimated for nonwhite males aged 20-24 in 1950 by Coale, using an iterative technique,[11] and these estimates are, in turn, similar to the undercount estimated for nonwhite males in 1940 by Price,[12] using Selective Service data. While consistency in the level of net census undercount over three censuses is not proof of the accuracy or validity of any one or all three of the estimates, it does suggest the reasonableness of the estimates. Confidence in the estimates is increased by the fact that the undercounts for the 1940 and 1960 censuses are based on two quite different methods and bodies of data.[13] In our opinion the high undercounts for nonwhite males in 1960 and concern with the possibility of inadequate matching in the tests do not provide sufficient reason for rejecting the results.

---

[11] A. J. Coale, op. cit.

[12] Daniel O. Price, "A Check on Underenumeration in the 1940 Census," American Sociological Review, Vol. XII (February 1947), pp. 44-49.

[13] Other grounds for accepting the official registration figures have been offered by A. J. Coale. He points out that if failure to match had represented a considerable part of what was considered underregistration, some of this would have occurred in hospital births, which, in fact, were nearly completely registered. He has also indicated that a study by J. T. Yamaguchi of the Princeton Office of Population Research, comparing the population as enumerated in 1960 by age, by geographic division of birth, with corresponding estimates for the census date based on births in each geographic division adjusted for underregistration, tends to confirm the high level of underregistration of births in 1940.

Method of Expected Sex Ratios. We have also employed another analytic technique for estimating net undercounts by age, sex, and color--namely, the application of "expected sex ratios." There are two problems involved in the use of this technique if it is to provide absolute estimates of adjusted population for both sexes. First, it requires an acceptable, independently determined, set of estimates of net undercounts, by age, for one sex. Second, the estimation of expected sex ratios involves a number of approximations which may lead to varying degrees of error. Both of these problems are more difficult to resolve in the case of nonwhites and the older population. We have completed the preparation of a set of expected sex ratios for the resident population, by age and color, which take account of the observed or estimated "actual" sex ratios of births, changing mortality by sex (represented by sex ratios of survival rates from various official life tables combined as quasi-generation life tables), excess war deaths, and the cumulative effects to 1960 of net civilian and military movement to and from the United States, by sex. These sex ratios are offered as more realistic than those serving the same purpose which are computed from a single sex ratio of births and a conventional life table for 1960.

The method assumes that the underregistration of births does not vary by sex and that the sex ratios of survival rates are not seriously affected by errors in the basic data used in constructing official life tables. In order to measure illustratively the effect of net census undercounts on the level of the sex ratios of survival rates, and hence on the level of expected sex ratios, the 1900

- 146 -

and 1960 life tables for Negroes or nonwhites were recalculated on the basis of the percentage net undercounts for 1960, and the resulting sex ratios of survival rates were compared with similar ratios based on unadjusted life tables. These computations indicate that the expected sex ratios would tend to be higher at most ages if the life tables were adjusted and that they are particularly sensitive to the level of the net undercounts at the older ages, where mortality rates are high.

A comparison of the expected sex ratios and the "enumerated" ratios in 1960 gives an indication of ratios lower than expected at all ages below 50, for whites and nonwhites separately, especially at ages 20 to 49 for nonwhites (see Table 5 for summary results). At ages above 55 the "enumerated" ratios are usually higher than expected, especially for nonwhites. (Adjustment of the expected sex ratios at these ages for a net census undercount does not bring them up to the level of the "enumerated" ratios, however.) The expected sex ratios agree quite closely with the sex ratios of the estimated population under 25 years of age, by age and color, based on births adjusted for underregistration, deaths, and net immigration. Estimates of the adjusted male population aged 25 and over in 1960, employing the sets of expected sex ratios, were derived from the analytic estimates for females and are shown in Table 2 (col. 3) and Table 3 (col. 6).

Estimates of Negro Population. Another analytic set of estimates of net undercounts is that prepared by Bogue and his associates for the Negro population by age and sex (Table 3, last col.).[14] We

---

[14]Bogue, Misra, and Dandekar, op. cit.

have given only limited attention to these estimates in our evaluation studies because, as the published critique by Zelnik indicates,[15] they suffer from a number of deficiencies. The methodology includes the use of an adjustment for age heaping to allow for net age-misreporting of grouped data (although the former type of adjustment is not particularly relevant to the latter problem), an (arbitrary) 2 percent estimate of net undercoverage by age, an additional (duplicate) allowance for net undercount of children under 10 based on births adjusted for underregistration, and use of a synthetic life table for 1960 to determine the sex ratios by age. The estimates of net undercounts arrived at by this procedure are generally lower than the other analytic estimates, with the outstanding exception at ages under 10. Coale has pointed out that Bogue's study has the highly doubtful implication that birth registration has been deteriorating.

Preferred Analytic Composite. Using the analytic techniques described so far, a set of estimates was defined representing a "preferred composite based on demographic analysis" (Table 6, cols. 3 and 4). The percentages of adjustment under age 25 by age and sex were derived from births adjusted for underregistration, carried forward with deaths and net immigration. The percentages for the white population aged 25 and over by age and sex were based on extensions to 1960 of the Coale-Zelnik estimates for 1950. The estimates for nonwhite females aged 25 and over by age were based on extensions to

---

[15] Melvin Zelnik, "An Evaluation of New Estimates of the Negro Population," Demography, Vol. 2 (1965), pp. 630-639.

1960 of the Coale estimates for 1950. The figures for nonwhite males were obtained by applying expected sex ratios to the nonwhite female population.

Results by Age, Sex, and Color. The differences among the alternative sets of estimates of net undercounts derived by demographic analysis, excluding the Bogue-Misra-Dandekar estimates, are small. Thus, the estimated net underenumeration for the total population is 3.1 or 3.2 percent, depending on the specific combination made of estimated net undercounts for the sex-color groups. For males, the estimates range from 3.8 to 4.0 percent and for females from 2.3 to 2.4 percent. These alternative sets of estimates yield the same estimate of net undercount for whites, 2.2 percent. For nonwhites, the estimates vary from 10.2 to 10.6 percent. All of these undercounts assume no change in the overall coverage of the 1950 and 1960 censuses (that is, a net immigration of 280,000 civilian citizens between 1950 and 1960).

The estimated net undercount for white females is 1.6 percent and for white males 2.8 or 2.9 percent. The differences between the two sexes are most pronounced from ages 15 to 49. At ages beyond this, females appear to be no better enumerated than males. The estimated undercounts for nonwhite males vary from 12.2 to 12.7 percent and for nonwhite females from 7.8 to 8.8 percent. The nonwhites show approximately the same pattern as the whites--smaller undercounts for females through the young adult ages, with smaller undercounts for males at the older ages.

There is wide variation in the estimates of net undercount for persons 65 and over, particularly for white and nonwhite males.

## Synthesis of Methods of Evaluation

Comparison of Results. We have described several sets of purely analytic estimates of net undercounts in the 1960 Census, and the Marks-Waksberg paper has described the estimates of coverage error derived from the record-matching studies and the reinterview studies. We should now like to consider these in relation to one another.

The results of the various methods for females, and particularly white females, are close, but the results for the other sex-color groups are quite different. (For this discussion, the analytic series principally referred to is the series identified as "preferred composite based on demographic analysis.") The comparative estimates of missed females are 1.8 percent for the reinterview method and 2.4 percent for the analytic method, and of missed males are 1.8 percent for the reinterview procedure and 3.9 percent for the analytic method. Both for males and females the discrepancy is much greater for nonwhites than for whites, although the figures for white males also differ significantly. For nonwhites as a whole, the respective figures are 3.8 percent and 10.5 percent. The estimate of net underenumeration of white females from the reinterview studies and the demographic analysis is virtually identical, 1.7 and 1.6 percent.

The relationships are much more erratic for individual age

groups.  Figures from the reinterview studies are affected not only by coverage errors but also by age-reporting errors and other problems of estimation, including sampling errors.  Although differences between the analytic estimates and the reinterview estimates (whether total net census error or net coverage error), considered in terms of broad age groups, are relatively small for white females, they are particularly great for white males in the age groups 15-29, 30-44, and 65 and over, for nonwhite males in all age groups except 5-14, and for nonwhite females under 5, 15-29, 45-64, and 65 and over.  In these cases, with the exception of the age group 65 and over, the analytic method shows the larger net undercounts.

Relative Limitations of Methods.  Each of the three methods of evaluation is subject to various limitations and varying degrees of error.  Reference was made to the limitations of the reinterview and record check studies in the paper by Marks and Waksberg.  In brief, the record check studies provide an impracticably wide range of estimates of the extent of gross underenumeration.  Allowing for gross overenumeration of 1.3 percent, the figures on net undercoverage range from 1.3 percent to 3.4 percent, depending on the assumptions made with regard to the coverage of persons for whom a definite determination about inclusion in the 1960 Census could not be made (16.5 percent of the sample).  The figures encompass the available estimates, although some narrowing of the range may be possible.

The analytic studies strongly suggest that the reinterview studies understate the overall coverage error for males and nonwhites. This deficiency applies in the case of all sex-color groups except white females.  The understatement of the error for nonwhite males by the reinterview studies is especially apparent in comparison with the "preferred analytic" estimates, but it remains evident even when the "analytic" estimates for males are derived by applying expected sex ratios to the female population adjusted by the net coverage error from the reinterview studies.  The 4 percent net underenumeration of nonwhite males from the reinterview studies compares with 12 percent and 7 percent from the analytic estimates referred to (Table 6, cols. 1, 3, and 5).  Some of the estimates of net coverage error by age are unreasonably low, for example, 0.1 percent for nonwhite males aged 15-29 and 1.2 percent for white males aged 15-29, or unreasonably high, for example, 6.7 percent for nonwhite males aged 65 and over.  Furthermore, the population sex ratios by age implied by the net coverage errors from the reinterview studies tend to be too low, particularly for nonwhites, although there are some striking "errors" in the opposite direction (Table 5, col. 5).

Marks and Waksberg caution against the use of the theoretically more appropriate estimates of net census errors (net coverage error combined with net age-misreporting error) from the reinterview studies on the ground that the age-misreporting-error component is subject to very large sampling errors and response biases, too large to add any information to that afforded by the net coverage error.  This component is also affected by the assumptions of the estimating method. Accordingly, we must generally rely on the net coverage error from the reinterview studies to represent the net census error; yet the net coverage error may substantially understate or overstate the net

census error if there is a pronounced bias in age reporting. The reliability of the net census errors should be greater for whites and
broader age groups.

The analytical approach also has its limitations. There is
considerable dependence of the estimates of net undercounts for persons under 25 on the results of the Birth Registration Tests in 1940
and 1950, and yet there is some uncertainty as to the accuracy of
these tests. Difficulties in matching the census records with birth
certificates would tend to cause an overstatement of the underregistration of births; and, as indicated earlier, the estimates of net
undercounts are quite sensitive to any errors in the correction for
underregistration. On the basis of the 1940 test results indicating
that 18 percent of nonwhite births were not registered, there is no
doubt that there was substantial underregistration of nonwhite births
in 1940, but there is a real question about the precise extent of
underregistration.

Next, the estimates of net undercounts for nonwhites above age
25 (that is, 1950 Coale estimates extended to 1960) depend heavily on
the assumption of similarity of the pattern of net undercounts at
successive recent censuses (1930, 1940, and 1950 in the Coale estimates) and on the estimates of net undercounts for children in these
censuses based on births adjusted for underregistration (under 15 in
the 1950 Coale estimates). The iterative technique has a tendency to
accumulate errors as one goes up the age scale, so that the estimates
for the older ages, particularly 65 and over, may be defective. Coale
himself rejected his original estimates for ages 65 and over.

Furthermore, the Census Bureau extension of the 1950 Coale-Zelnik estimates of net undercounts for whites above age 25 in 1960 may be questioned on a number of grounds. There is, first, the acceptability of the fundamental assumptions from which the basic estimates were derived in 1950, particularly the assumption of a common level of net undercount for females aged 15-29 in each prior census. Further questions relate to the procedure of estimating population by age in 1950 after the historical series of birth estimates was determined, the procedure of extending the estimates for native whites in 1950 to include the foreign born, and, as in general, the adequacy of the estimates of intercensal change by which the adjusted population in 1950 was carried to 1960.

Composite Estimates Based on Reinterview Studies and Demographic Analysis. Despite these limitations, we want to take advantage of these various estimates to develop a set or sets of estimates of population for April 1, 1960, by age, sex, and color, that would be significantly more accurate than the 1960 Census statistics and that could be recommended for general use.

A number of possible criteria for such estimates may be identified. A single set of "best" estimates of net undercounts may be sought. On the other hand, it may be preferable to try to establish a range, giving high and low estimates, or minimum and maximum estimates, of net undercounts. These could be developed in combination with, or independently of, a set of "best" estimates. The range would suggest the degree of uncertainty associated with the estimates of net undercount, although no specific mathematical probabilities could be assigned to the high and low figures. The calculation of alternative estimates has certain limitations and certain advantages. Offering alternative estimates presents certain practical difficulties to many users, who prefer a single set of figures; on the other hand, the availability of a set of high and low figures makes possible a choice by the user in conformity with a cost analysis of his problem, which may call for a high or a low figure. He will often prefer the high series, particularly if this is consistent with maximum costs. On the other hand, the high estimates involve the risk of deviating from the true figure more than the census counts do, that is, they involve the risk of serious overstatement. In fact, it may be considered desirable to avoid overstatement altogether and to develop a set of adjustments, which may be regarded with a high degree of certainty as being understatements of the errors in the census counts and yet as the largest acceptable estimates of error. As lower bounds of the true figures or "minimum reasonable" estimates, such figures may be described as representing a highly conservative choice of a single set of best estimates.

A few experimental sets of estimates of this kind have been prepared. The starting point for the first set is the estimate of net coverage error for white females obtained from the reinterview studies and the demographic analyses. As noted, the estimate is virtually identical in both sources: 1.7 or 1.6 percent of the census count. The estimated errors for white females differ somewhat by age group in the two series, however. The estimates of net coverage error from the reinterview studies--which are remarkably constant up to age 45 and approximately so throughout the age distribution--were adopted. Thus, estimates of the total number of white females in the United States by age were obtained from the reinterview studies. Since we are attempting to understate the net error, the estimates of nonwhite females derived from the reinterview studies were used in the same way (3.4 percent at all ages as compared with 8.8 percent from the demographic analyses). To derive estimates of the adjusted male population, expected sex ratios were applied to the estimates of ad-justed female population. The results are shown in broad age groups in Table 6 (set 1). The resulting net errors for white males are 3.0 percent, for nonwhite males, 6.7 percent, and for the total population, 2.6 percent. The use of expected sex ratios gives a net undercount for white males that is 1.3 percentage points greater than for white females and 3.3 percentage points greater for nonwhite males than for nonwhite females. The resulting figures for males exceed the net cov-erage errors of the reinterview studies in most age groups, and hence are not minimal in relation to the available estimates. However, the net coverage errors for males from the reinterview studies are, for the most part, untenably low now not only in relation to the figures for males obtained from the adjusted figures for females and expected sex ratios but also in relation to the net coverage errors for females.

The second set of composite estimates of net undercounts (whites only) also makes use of the fact that the overall net coverage error for white females obtained in the reinterview studies is about the same as the figure shown by the analytic studies. In these calculations, estimates of the population under 25 years of age based on adjusted births, deaths, and net immigration were combined with estimates for females aged 25 and over consistent with an all-ages coverage error of 1.6 percent for females; and estimates for males aged 25 and over were then derived from the estimates for females by use of expected sex ratios. These calculations also happen to imply a net coverage error of 1.6 percent for the white female population aged 25 and over. Females were assigned the net census errors (net coverage error plus net age-reporting error) from the reinterview studies for very broad age groups (Series A, ages 25-44, 45-64, and 65 and over; Series B, ages 25-34, 35-44, 45-54, and 55 and over), and the figures so adjusted were distributed into smaller age groups on the basis of the "demographic" estimates. The resulting estimates of error are shown in Table 6 (set 2). The net error for white males is 2.9 percent.

Still another approximation to "conservative best" estimates or "minimum reasonable" estimates are given as set 3 in Table 6. In this set the demographic estimates of net undercounts based on adjusted births, deaths, and net immigration were accepted only for ages under 15 (under 5 and 5-14).[16] This choice implies sufficient confidence in the results of the 1950 Birth Registration Test to accept the estimates based on births since 1945 but not sufficient confidence in the results of the 1940 Test to accept the estimates based on earlier

---

[16] For whites these were generally lower than the estimates of net coverage error; for nonwhites they were higher.

births.[17] For the next three older groups of females, 15-29, 30-44, and 45-64, we selected the smaller figure as between the estimates of net undercount from the demographic analyses and the net coverage error from the reinterview studies. Accordingly, all figures came from the reinterview studies except that for white females 30-44 years of age. For this group, the figure selected was quite small, 0.1 percent, but it agrees with the net census error from the reinterview studies. Estimates of net undercounts for males were derived by applying expected sex ratios to the adjusted figures for females. To complete this set of estimates, the population aged 65 and over, for whites and nonwhites, was assumed to have no net error since we have been unable to establish whether the census counts overstated or understated the population. The census counts were then divided by sex on the basis of expected sex ratios.

Estimates for males so calculated are often well above the coverage errors for males from the reinterview studies. This set of figures shows net errors of 2.4 percent for white males, 1.1 percent for white females, 8.0 percent for nonwhite males, and 4.7 percent for nonwhite females (Table 6, set 3). These levels of net error are somewhat lower for white males and females, and somewhat higher for nonwhite males and females, than the levels indicated by the composite estimates based on both demographic analysis and reinterview studies previously computed (that is, sets 1 and 2 of Table 6). The

---

[17]This is an arbitrary choice, since 1945 does not represent a turning point in the improvement of birth registration; rather, improvement was gradual during the forties.

overall level of net underenumeration in 1960, 2.2 percent, is roughly the same as the figure expected on the basis of the Census Bureau's "minimum reasonable" estimate of 2.5 percent for 1950.

There is a logical weakness to this procedure because it is unlikely that the net error for all nonwhites aged 65 and over is zero while nonwhite males are substantially overstated (6 percent) and nonwhite females are substantially understated (5 percent). If, on the other hand, the census counts for both sex groups are taken without adjustment, the implied sex ratio for nonwhites is quite unreasonable (90 as compared with an expected value of 80).

Of course, many other sets of composite estimates of net undercounts, designed to represent conservative estimates, are possible. One could accept the "preferred composite based on demographic analysis" as the best estimates, and reduce these by a fixed proportion, say one third or one quarter, to derive a set of conservative best estimates. However, this procedure would give estimates for white females below those from the reinterview studies and estimates for ages under 25 below those based on adjusted births.

The various composite series described here would not necessarily increase the accuracy of the relative distribution by age, for the census date. Furthermore, the changes by age since the census date, implied by current estimates of population adjusted on the basis of the composite estimates of net census undercounts, would not necessarily be more realistic than if the data had not been adjusted. These limitations result from the fact that the proportion of the actual net undercounts allowed for in these composite estimates varies from age to age. On the other hand, the absolute level of the adjusted census counts or current estimates at each age (except possibly at ages 65 and over) would be closer to the theoretical truth.

Differential Coverage. One of the main reasons for the concern about the extent of coverage error in censuses stems from the fact that it varies widely among groups of the population (age, sex, color, socioeconomic status, etc.) and geographic areas in the country (states, cities, counties, urban-rural, etc.). If the level of coverage error were the same among all population groups and geographic areas, there would be less need for and concern about the availability of estimates of coverage error.

In general, we believe that coverage error contributes more heavily to the anomalies of the census counts by age, sex, and color than errors of age reporting. Therefore, we are less concerned about age-reporting errors than undercoverage for most of the age distribution; possibly at ages over 50, age-reporting errors become relatively important and may dominate.

Our studies of the quality of the 1960 Census data have indicated the following differences in coverage:

1. The enumeration of males is less complete than that of females, at least up until ages 45 or 50.

2. The enumeration of nonwhites is substantially less complete than that of whites, probably at all ages but certainly until age 60 or 65.

3.  The enumeration of males at ages 15 through 44, especially

for nonwhites, is less complete than at other ages or the av-

erage level over all ages.  The population under age 5 is no

longer to be singled out as a group with especially bad cov-

erage.

In addition, by inference from the 1960 reinterview studies and

from the results of the 1950 Post-Enumeration Survey, we may make the

following conclusions:

1.  There are important geographic variations in the complete-

ness of enumeration.  Coverage is probably poorer in the central

cities of our metropolitan areas than in the suburban counties,

and probably poorer in the South than in the rest of the United

States.  Coverage is probably poorest in the slum areas of our

big cities, but we do not have evidence from interview or other

studies to support this conclusion.

2.  The underenumeration of young children (children under 5

years of age) is very probably closely related to the under-

enumeration of their parents.  According to the Infant Enumer-

ation Study of 1950, in 80 percent of the cases where infants

were missed their parents were also missed.[18]

Age-Reporting Errors.  Because of the limitations of the record-

matching studies and the reinterview studies, we have little basis for

--------------------

[18]U. S. Bureau of the Census, Infant Enumeration Study:  1950,
Procedural Studies of the 1950 Censuses, No. 1 (1953).

describing the pattern of age-reporting errors in the 1960 Census. Two estimates are available: (1) estimates based directly on the reinterview studies and (2) estimates derived by taking the difference between the net undercounts based on demographic analysis and the net coverage errors from the reinterview studies. Reference has already been made to the inadequacies of the former estimates arising from sampling error, response biases, and the assumptions in the estimating method. The lack of comparability of the components of the second estimate and the limitations of each component have also been noted. The estimates for white females alone may be informative. In short, we do not have any solid facts about the age-reporting errors in the 1960 Census.

There is some evidence, although far from conclusive (for example, the residual estimates for the population aged 65 and over for the 1950-1960 decade), to suggest that the 1960 Census may contain a net overstatement of persons aged 65 years and over. This overstatement is accompanied by an understatement, arising from age-reporting errors, in the age groups that immediately precede the 65-and-over group. However, as of now, we do not know the extent, or even the direction, of error in the census count for ages 65 and over. Further research may clarify this question.

Conclusion. In conclusion, we know little in a formal manner regarding the reasons for underenumeration or the geographic variations in coverage error, and we have only rough or approximate measures of net census errors by age, sex, and color. We continue to have considerable concern about the validity of the differences by color and by age shown by the available estimates of net coverage error or net census error. We have greater confidence in the validity of our estimates of the differences by sex.

We have developed a number of sets of estimates of net under-counts by age, sex, and color, some involving a synthesis of methods and techniques, but we have so far been unable to arrive at a single set of figures that we feel we can recommend for general use. Efforts along these lines will continue with the hope of achieving this goal.

Table 1. ESTIMATED PERCENTAGE OF NET UNDERENUMERATION IN 1960, FOR VARIOUS PERCENTAGES OF NET UNDERENUMERATION IN 1950 AND VARIOUS ABSOLUTE AMOUNTS OF CHANGE IN COVERAGE BETWEEN 1950 AND 1960

(Percentage base is census count of resident population.)

| 1950 Source | Percentage Net Under-enumeration | 1960 Percentage Net Underenumeration According to 1950-1960 Change in Coverage | | | |
|---|---|---|---|---|---|
| | | No Change in Coverage | Coverage Increase of 277,000 | Coverage Decrease of 403,000 | Coverage Increase of 449,000 |
| PES estimate[1] | 1.4 | 1.2 | 1.0 | 1.4 | 0.9 |
| Minimum reasonable estimate[1] | 2.5 | 2.1 | 1.9 | 2.3 | 1.8 |
| Arbitrary 3 percent | 3.0 | 2.5 | 2.4 | 2.8 | 2.3 |
| Coale estimate[2] | 3.6 | 3.0 | 2.9 | 3.3 | 2.8 |

[1] U. S. Bureau of the Census, The Post-Enumeration Survey: 1950, Technical Paper No. 4 (1960).

[2] Ansley J. Coale, "The Population of the United States in 1950 Classified by Age, Sex, and Color--A Revision of Census Figures," Journal of the American Statistical Association, Vol. 50 (March 1955), pp. 16-54.

Table 2. ESTIMATES OF PERCENTAGE NET CENSUS UNDERCOUNT OF THE WHITE
POPULATION, BASED ON ANALYTIC AND COMPOSITE METHODS,
BY AGE AND SEX: 1950 AND 1960

(Percentage base is census count of resident population;
a minus sign denotes net census overcount.)

| Sex and Age | 1950 Series P-25, No. 310[1] | 1960 Series P-25, No. 310[2] A[3] | 1960 Series P-25, No. 310[2] B[4] | 1960 Composite Estimate[5] A | 1960 Composite Estimate[5] B |
|---|---|---|---|---|---|
| Male, all ages | 3.2 | 2.8 | 2.9 | 2.9 | 2.9 |
| Under 5 | 4.5 | 2.0 | 2.0 | 2.0 | 2.0 |
| 5-9 | 3.1 | 2.5 | 2.5 | 2.5 | 2.5 |
| 10-14 | 1.0 | 2.6 | 2.6 | 2.6 | 2.6 |
| 15-19 | 4.2 | 4.0 | 4.0 | 4.0 | 4.0 |
| 20-24 | 5.9 | 4.5 | 4.5 | 4.5 | 4.5 |
| 25-29 | 5.2 | 4.9 | 4.4 | 4.9 | 4.7 |
| 30-34 | 4.5 | 5.1 | 3.2 | 3.7 | 3.5 |
| 35-39 | 2.1 | 4.8 | 2.6 | 3.1 | 3.3 |
| 40-44 | 3.4 | 3.5 | 1.9 | 2.4 | 2.6 |
| 45-49 | 2.2 | 2.5 | 1.6 | 0.7 | -0.1 |
| 50-54 | 2.2 | 4.4 | 3.7 | 2.7 | 2.0 |
| 55-59 | 5.3 | 0.7 | 0.4 | -0.6 | 0.7 |
| 60-64 | 3.6 | 3.6 | 3.1 | 2.1 | 3.4 |
| 65 and over | -2.0 | -3.4 | 4.0 | 4.7 | 4.4 |
| Female, all ages | 2.1 | 1.6 | | 1.6 | 1.6 |
| Under 5 | 3.8 | 1.2 | | 1.2 | 1.2 |
| 5-9 | 2.5 | 1.6 | | 1.6 | 1.6 |
| 10-14 | 1.1 | 1.5 | | 1.5 | 1.5 |
| 15-19 | 1.8 | 2.5 | | 2.5 | 2.5 |
| 20-24 | 1.6 | 2.5 | | 2.5 | 2.5 |
| 25-29 | 0.3 | 1.4 | | 1.9 | 1.7 |
| 30-34 | 0.1 | 0.6 | | 1.1 | 0.9 |
| 35-39 | -1.4 | -0.2 | | 0.2 | 0.4 |
| 40-44 | 2.0 | -0.2 | | 0.3 | 0.4 |
| 45-49 | 1.5 | 0.7 | | -0.3 | -1.0 |
| 50-54 | 2.7 | 4.4 | | 3.4 | 2.7 |
| 55-59 | 7.6 | 1.6 | | 0.7 | 2.0 |
| 60-64 | 7.3 | 4.4 | | 3.4 | 4.7 |
| 65 and over | 2.3 | 2.1 | | 2.8 | 2.5 |

(continued.)

Table 2 (<u>continued</u>).

---

[1]U. S. Bureau of the Census, <u>Current Population Reports</u>, Series P-25, No. 310 (1965). Figures relate to resident population of the United States. Estimates under age 15: Based on adjusted births, deaths, and net immigration data. Estimates for age 15 and over: Based on Coale-Zelnik estimates for native whites.

[2]Estimates under age 25: Based on adjusted births, deaths, and net immigration data.

[3]Estimates for ages 25 and over, for males and females, are extensions to 1960 of Coale-Zelnik estimates for 1950.

[4]Males aged 25 and over: Expected sex ratios applied to adjusted female population.

[5]Males and females under age 25: Based on adjusted births, deaths, and net immigration data. Males aged 25 and over: Expected sex ratios applied to adjusted female population. Females aged 25 and over: Adjusted for net <u>census</u> error in broad age groups, as indicated by reinterview studies, consistent with an all-ages net <u>coverage</u> error of 1.6 percent and a uniform net <u>coverage</u> error of 1.6 percent for ages 25 and over by age. Percentage redistribution of females into 5-year age groups in alternative series based on:
  A. Distribution within age groups 25-44 and 45-64 from P-25, No. 310.
  B. Distribution within age groups 25-34, 35-44, 45-54, and 55 and over from P-25, No. 310.

Table 3. ESTIMATES OF PERCENTAGE NET CENSUS UNDERCOUNT OF THE NONWHITE POPULATION, BASED ON ANALYTIC AND COMPOSITE METHODS, BY AGE AND SEX: 1950 AND 1960

(Percentage base is census count of resident population; a minus sign denotes net census overcount.)

| Sex and Age | 1950 | | | 1960 | | | |
| | P-25, No. 310[1] | Coale[2] | Bogue et al.[3] | P-25, No. 310[1] | 1950 Coale Estimates Extended to 1960[4] | | Bogue et al.[3] |
| | | | | | A[5] | B[6] | |
| Male, all ages | 14.8 | 15.0 | 8.8 | 12.7 | 12.6 | 12.2 | 8.9 |
| Under 5 | 11.1 | 11.0 | 8.9 | 8.4 | 8.4 | 8.4 | 11.0 |
| 5-9 | 11.9 | 12.0 | 2.8 | 6.0 | 6.0 | 6.0 | 8.9 |
| 10-14 | 6.6 | 7.0 | * | 5.5 | 5.5 | 5.5 | 3.0 |
| 15-19 | 15.3 | 18.0 | 11.7 | 14.3 | 14.3 | 14.3 | 4.7 |
| 20-24 | 19.0 | 19.0 | 22.6 | 21.2 | 21.2 | 21.2 | 16.8 |
| 25-29 | 24.9 | 20.0 | 19.5 | 18.9 | 21.7 | 24.5 | 17.7 |
| 30-34 | 34.4 | 20.0 | 19.2 | 16.0 | 16.0 | 22.0 | 18.7 |
| 35-39 | 19.6 | 12.0 | 6.3 | 22.7 | 17.8 | 16.9 | 16.9 |
| 40-44 | 13.6 | 20.0 | 5.3 | 28.8 | 14.4 | 14.6 | 12.8 |
| 45-49 | 16.4 | 13.0 | 4.8 | 21.8 | 13.5 | 13.1 | 7.4 |
| 50-54 | 14.8 | 11.0 | 8.3 | 15.5 | 22.8 | 21.7 | 6.2 |
| 55-59 | 18.0 | 17.0 | 17.3 | 13.3 | 9.3 | 6.3 | -2.0 |
| 60-64 | 17.1 | 24.0 | 20.2 | 18.5 | 13.5 | 10.6 | 10.6 |
| 65 and over | -13.7 | 12.0 | -15.7 | -9.2 | 12.2 | 1.9 | -10.1 |

(continued.)

Table 3 (<u>continued</u>).

| Sex and Age | 1950 | | | 1960 | | | |
|---|---|---|---|---|---|---|---|
| | P-25, No. 310[1] | Coale[2] | Bogue et al.[3] | P-25, No. 310[1] | 1950 Coale Estimates Extended to 1960[4] | | Bogue et al.[3] |
| | | | | | A[5] | B[6] | |
| Female, all ages | 9.5 | 11.0 | 3.5 | 7.8 | 8.8 ⎫ | | 3.8 |
| Under 5 | 10.3 | 10.0 | 7.6 | 6.8 | 6.8 | | 9.8 |
| 5-9 | 9.7 | 10.0 | 0.3 | 5.1 | 5.1 | | 8.1 |
| 10-14 | 7.0 | 7.0 | -1.7 | 4.4 | 4.4 | | 2.1 |
| 15-19 | 8.7 | 12.0 | 3.4 | 11.2 | 11.2 | | 1.3 |
| 20-24 | 2.6 | 8.0 | 3.3 | 10.7 | 10.7 | | 2.7 |
| 25-29 | 6.7 | 8.0 | 4.3 | 6.4 | 9.6 | | 2.2 |
| 30-34 | 8.6 | 9.0 | 4.3 | 1.0 | 6.3 | | 1.5 |
| 35-39 | 2.2 | 3.0 | -5.2 | 5.4 | 6.7 | | 3.3 |
| 40-44 | 5.6 | 18.0 | 1.1 | 6.4 | 6.8 | | 1.3 |
| 45-49 | 12.3 | 12.0 | 2.8 | 8.3 | 9.2 | | * |
| 50-54 | 19.6 | 16.0 | 12.4 | 8.3 | 22.3 | | 2.7 |
| 55-59 | 35.0 | 30.0 | 30.9 | 11.5 | 11.1 | | -1.3 |
| 60-64 | 36.4 | 36.0 | 36.4 | 20.9 | 16.5 | | 10.8 |
| 65 and over | 6.5 | 5.0 | -14.4 | 17.2 | 14.0 | | 0.8 |

(continued.)

Table 3 (continued).

*Zero or a rounding to zero.

[1]U. S. Bureau of the Census, Current Population Reports, Series P-25, No. 310 (1965). Figures relate to the resident population of the United States.

[2]A. J. Coale, "The Population of the United States in 1950 . . . Revision of Census Figures," op. cit. Figures relate to resident population of conterminous United States.

[3]D. J. Bogue, B. D. Misra, and D. P. Dandekar, "A New Estimate of the Negro Population and Negro Vital Rates in the United States, 1930-1960," Demography, Vol. I (1964). Figures relate to resident Negro population of conterminous United States.

[4]Estimates under age 25: Based on adjusted births, deaths, and net immigration data.

[5]Males and females aged 25 and over: 1950 Coale estimates carried forward to 1960 by estimate of intercensal change given in Series P-25, No. 310.

[6]Males aged 25 and over: Expected sex ratios applied to adjusted female population for 1960.

- 169 -

Table 4.   ESTIMATED PERCENTAGES OF NET CENSUS UNDERCOUNT FOR THE
POPULATION UNDER 25 YEARS OF AGE, BY AGE, COLOR,
AND SEX, BASED ON ADJUSTED BIRTHS:   1960

(Percentage base is census count of resident population.)

| Color and Age | Official Factors for Underregistration of Births | | Assuming One-Third Reduction in Under-registration of Births | |
|---|---|---|---|---|
| | Male | Female | Male | Female |
| White | | | | |
| Under 5 | 2.0 | 1.2 | 1.7 | 0.9 |
| 5-9 | 2.5 | 1.6 | 2.1 | 1.3 |
| 10-14 | 2.6 | 1.5 | 1.9 | 0.9 |
| 15-19 | 4.0 | 2.5 | 2.0 | 0.6 |
| 20-24 | 4.5 | 2.5 | 1.5 | 0.1 |
| Nonwhite | | | | |
| Under 5 | 8.4 | 6.8 | 6.9 | 5.2 |
| 5-9 | 6.0 | 5.1 | 3.9 | 3.1 |
| 10-14 | 5.5 | 4.4 | 1.7 | 0.8 |
| 15-19 | 14.3 | 11.2 | 6.3 | 3.8 |
| 20-24 | 21.2 | 10.7 | 10.6 | 1.8 |

Table 5.  COMPARISON OF "ENUMERATED" AND EXPECTED SEX RATIOS WITH SEX RATIOS OF ADJUSTED POPULATIONS, BY BROAD AGE GROUPS AND COLOR: 1960

(Males per 100 females in resident population.)

| Age and Color | "Enumerated" Sex Ratios | Expected Sex Ratios | Sex Ratios Based on Population Adjusted by—[1] | | | | |
| --- | --- | --- | --- | --- | --- | --- | --- |
| | | | Net Coverage Error from Reinterview Studies | Preferred Composite Based on Demographic Analysis | Composite Based on Reinterview Studies and Demographic Analysis | | |
| | | | | | Set 1 | Set 2 | Set 3 |
| WHITE | | | | | | | |
| All ages | 97.4 | 98.6 | 97.3 | 98.5 | 98.6 | 98.6 | 98.7 |
| Under 5 | 104.0 | 104.8 | 103.6 | 104.8 | 104.8 | 104.8 | 104.8 |
| 5-14 | 103.9 | 104.9 | 102.9 | 104.9 | 104.9 | 104.9 | 104.9 |
| 15-29 | 98.5 | 100.8 | 98.2 | 100.7 | 100.8 | 100.6 | 100.8 |
| 30-44 | 96.4 | 98.8 | 96.1 | 100.6 | 98.8 | 98.8 | 98.8 |
| 45-64 | 95.6 | 95.2 | 96.5 | 95.8 | 95.2 | 95.2 | 95.2 |
| 65 and over | 82.3 | 83.8 | 83.1 | 77.8 | 83.8 | 83.8 | 83.8 |
| NONWHITE | | | | | | | |
| All ages | 94.7 | 97.6 | 95.4 | 97.6 | 97.6 | * | 97.7 |
| Under 5 | 99.9 | 101.4 | 100.7 | 101.5 | 101.4 | * | 101.5 |
| 5-14 | 100.0 | 100.9 | 101.3 | 101.0 | 100.9 | * | 101.0 |
| 15-29 | 91.6 | 98.7 | 89.6 | 99.1 | 98.7 | * | 98.7 |
| 30-44 | 88.4 | 97.9 | 89.7 | 97.8 | 97.9 | * | 97.9 |
| 45-64 | 95.8 | 95.0 | 97.1 | 94.9 | 95.0 | * | 95.0 |
| 65 and over | 90.1 | 80.5 | 94.4 | 80.5 | 80.5 | * | 80.5 |

*Not applicable.

[1] See footnotes to Tables 2, 3, and 6 for an explanation of the basis for the adjusted figures.

Table 6. ESTIMATED PERCENTAGES OF NET COVERAGE ERROR AND OF NET CENSUS UNDERCOUNTS BASED ON ANALYTIC AND COMPOSITE METHODS, BY SEX, COLOR, AND BROAD AGE GROUPS: 1960

(Percentage base is census count of resident population; a minus sign denotes net census overcount.)

| Age and Color | Net Coverage Error from Reinterview Studies[1] | | Preferred Composite Based on Demographic Analysis[2] | | Composite Based on Reinterview Studies and Demographic Analysis[3] | | | | | |
| | | | | | Set 1[4] | | Set 2[5] | | Set 3[6] | |
| | Male | Female | Male | Female | Male | Female | Male | Female | Male | Female |
|---|---|---|---|---|---|---|---|---|---|---|
| **WHITE** | | | | | | | | | | |
| All ages | 1.6 | 1.7 | 2.8 | 1.6 | 3.0 | 1.7 | 2.9 | 1.6 | 2.4 | 1.1 |
| Under 5 | 1.3 | 1.7 | 2.0 | 1.2 | 2.5 | 1.7 | 2.0 | 1.2 | 2.0 | 1.2 |
| 5-14 | 0.6 | 1.6 | 2.5 | 1.6 | 2.5 | 1.6 | 2.5 | 1.6 | 2.5 | 1.6 |
| 15-29 | 1.2 | 1.6 | 4.5 | 2.2 | 3.9 | 1.6 | 4.4 | 2.3 | 3.9 | 1.6 |
| 30-44 | 1.3 | 1.6 | 4.5 | 0.1 | 4.2 | 1.6 | 3.1 | 0.6 | 2.6 | 0.1 |
| 45-64 | 2.8 | 1.9 | 2.8 | 2.6 | 1.4 | 1.9 | 1.4 | 1.8 | 1.4 | 1.9 |
| 65 and over | 2.3 | 1.3 | -3.4 | 2.1 | 3.1 | 1.3 | 4.4 | 2.5 | 1.0 | -0.8 |
| **NONWHITE** | | | | | | | | | | |
| All ages | 4.2 | 3.4 | 12.2 | 8.8 | 6.7 | 3.4 | * | * | 8.0 | 4.7 |
| Under 5 | 2.6 | 1.8 | 8.4 | 6.8 | 3.3 | 1.8 | * | * | 8.4 | 6.8 |
| 5-14 | 4.6 | 3.3 | 5.8 | 4.8 | 4.1 | 3.3 | * | * | 5.8 | 4.8 |
| 15-29 | 0.1 | 2.5 | 19.5 | 10.6 | 10.3 | 2.5 | * | * | 10.4 | 2.5 |
| 30-44 | 5.8 | 4.2 | 18.0 | 6.6 | 15.3 | 4.2 | * | * | 15.4 | 4.2 |
| 45-64 | 7.3 | 5.9 | 13.4 | 14.4 | 5.0 | 5.9 | * | * | 5.0 | 5.9 |
| 65 and over | 6.7 | 1.8 | 1.9 | 14.0 | -8.9 | 1.8 | * | * | -5.9 | 5.3 |

(continued.)

Table 6 (continued).

*Not applicable.

[1]Based on reinterview studies EP-8 and EP-9.

[2]Whites and nonwhites under age 25: Consistent with percentages of net undercount in Series P-25, No. 310 (based on adjusted births, deaths, and net immigration data). Whites aged 25 and over: Consistent with percentages of net undercount in Current Population Reports, Series P-25, No. 310 (Coale-Zelnik estimates for 1950 extended to 1960). Nonwhite females aged 25 and over: Coale estimates for 1950 extended to 1960. Nonwhite males aged 25 and over: Expected sex ratios applied to the adjusted female population.

[3]Lower bounds of true errors or "minimum reasonable" estimates.

[4]Females: Net coverage error from the reinterview studies. Males: Expected sex ratios applied to the adjusted female population.

[5]Males and females under age 25: Based on adjusted births, deaths, and net immigration data. Females aged 25 and over: Adjusted for net census error in broad age groups as indicated by reinterview studies, consistent with an all-ages net coverage error of 1.6 percent and a uniform net coverage error of 1.6 percent for ages 25 and over by age. Males aged 25 and over: Expected sex ratios applied to adjusted female population. Estimates correspond to detailed estimates labeled "Composite Estimates B," Table 2.

[6]Males and females under age 15: Based on adjusted births, deaths, and net immigration data. Females aged 15-64: Net coverage error from reinterview studies or preferred composite based on demographic analysis, whichever is lower. Males aged 15-64: Expected sex ratios applied to adjusted female population. Population aged 65 and over: Census counts by color, distributed by sex on the basis of expected sex ratios.

RESOLUTIONS OF THE CONFERENCE

The Conference on Social Statistics and the City, convened by the Joint Center for Urban Studies of the Massachusetts Institute of Technology and Harvard University, meeting in Washington, D. C., June 22-23, 1967, by general concurrence resolved the following:

## Improving Enumeration of Negroes, Puerto Ricans, and Mexicans

1. While American population statistics are among the very finest in the world, papers presented to the Conference have established beyond reasonable doubt that the Decennial Census, the Current Population Survey, and to a lesser degree, the Vital Statistics of the United States, seriously and significantly underenumerate or underestimate the size of the Negro, Puerto Rican, and Mexican American populations. As much as 10 percent of the Negro population may not have been counted in the 1960 Census, and there is considerable probability that the Puerto Ricans and Mexican Americans were similarly undercounted.

In 1960 as many as one Negro male in six within the age group 20-39 may have been omitted altogether.

In a modern society statistical information is not only a primary guide to public and private actions, in itself it profoundly influences patterns of thought and basic assumptions as to the way things are and the way they are likely to be. Were national statistics merely inadequate, but uniformly so, the nation would be at a disadvantage, but no special injury could be claimed by any region or group. As it happens, however, where American population statistics are inadequate, they will normally be found to be so in terms of the underenumeration and underestimation of minority groups, defined in terms of race or national origin, and concentrated in specific neighborhoods, usually in densely populated central city areas. They are also, characteristically, defined by poverty. But a larger issue than that simply of efficiency and convenience must enter into a consideration of this subject. A constitutional issue is involved.

Article I, Section 3, of the Constitution provides for the enumeration once each ten years of all persons residing within the United States. This enumeration is explicitly and primarily designed to provide the basis for representation in the House of Representatives. In the years since the adoption of the Constitution, the Census enumeration and other statistical programs, such as those conducted by the Bureau of Labor Statistics, have come to be the basis for a host of public activities; and most particularly they provide the basis on which public funds are allocated in a whole range of government programs at the national, state, and local level. In some cases funds are allocated on a straight "head count" basis. In other cases, for example under the Economic Development Act, Title I of the Elementary and Secondary Education Act, and in the Model Cities legislation, public funds are allocated on the basis of population together with a range of special economic and other information collected by government agencies.

The record of these agencies, notably the Bureau of the Census, in gathering and compiling this information with the highest technical competence, the utmost standards of impartiality and integrity, and at the most modest cost is a matter of national pride. Typically it has been the Census Bureau itself that has been the most diligent in discovering and analyzing the problems of gathering statistics relating to minority groups.

Nonetheless, the problem of underenumeration of minority groups is likely to persist unless it becomes a matter of more general concern. We believe that what, initially at least, were technical problems have by their very magnitude been transformed into social problems with powerful legal and ethical implications. Specifically, we hold that where a group defined by racial or ethnic terms, and concentrated in specific political jurisdictions, is significantly undercounted in relation to other groups, then individual members of that group are thereby deprived of the constitutional right to equal representation in the House of Representatives and, by inference, in other legislative bodies. Further, we hold that individual members of such a group are thereby deprived of their right to equal protection of the laws as provided by Section I of the 14th Amendment to the Constitution in that they are deprived of their entitlement to partake in federal and other programs designed for areas and populations with their characteristics.

Injury, while general, is real; redress is in order. This would seem a matter of special concern to the nation in view of recent Supreme Court rulings establishing the "one man, one vote" principle in apportioning legislatures and in view of the extensive Congressional activity in the establishment of programs designed to improve the economic and social status of just those groups that appear to be substantially underrepresented in our current population statistics.

The Bureau of the Census and other government statistical agencies have set a superb standard of public accountability by themselves calling attention to this problem. We feel it is incumbent on the Congress to provide the Bureau of the Census, the National Center of Health Statistics, the Bureau of Labor Statistics, and such other agencies as are concerned, with the funds necessary to obtain a full enumeration of all groups in the population, and also to gather the usual information on special and economic characteristics that is necessary to implement the laws of the nation.

2. The Conference likewise emphasizes that there is an obligation on the part of every resident to be enumerated.

3. The Conference commends the Bureau of the Census for the innovative use of the Post Office to ensure a more complete enumeration. The Conference believes that the Post Office will contribute to the improvement of the coverage of the census not only in general but particularly in the central cities.

4. The Conference wishes to encourage the Bureau of the Census to explore more flexible personnel procedures from the standpoint, first, of enlarging the number of people who can be located to serve usefully as regular enumerators and, second, of employing people in various auxiliary roles to help ensure completeness of count.

5.  The Bureau of the Census, working in concert with other groups, public and private, should work to develop enumerator skills, particularly for conditions in the central cities, and to instill a professional spirit among enumerators.

6.  The Conference suggests consideration of the appointment of enumerators or supervisors by Presidential commission as a means of impressing them with the seriousness of the task.

7.  The Conference wishes to encourage the Bureau of the Census to take an experimental approach toward the use of various incentives for respondents.

8.  The Conference is impressed with the extent to which improvements in closeout procedures[*] and procedures for following back to apparently vacant housing units may contribute to the reduction of underenumeration. We put high priority, therefore, on changes in procedures and in the allocation of resources that promise an improvement in this area.

9.  The Conference would like to urge financial support for further studies of underenumeration in the 1970 Census, such as the study of 1960 underenumeration by Jacob Siegel, extended to specific estimates of underenumeration by age, sex, race, ethnic group, and residence.

_____

[*]Closeout procedures determine the number of calls an enumerator must make at a particular household in an attempt to gather information. If no information can be gathered after the specified number of calls, characteristics of the household are allocated by a computer.

## Improving Vital Statistics for Negroes, Puerto Ricans, and Mexicans

1. We recommend that the Bureau of the Census and the National Center for Health Statistics study methods for improving the completeness and quality of Census data to enable the computation of vital rates for minority groups, particularly those groups which have been included with the white population in the past.

2. We recommend that the National Center for Health Statistics, through the mechanisms of the Public Health Conference on Records and Statistics and the American Association of Vital Registrars and Public Health Statisticians, ask state and local health departments to make more tabulations and classifications of vital records for minority groups.

3. We recommend that the National Center for Health Statistics make known what material the state and local health agencies collect, tabulate, and publish concerning vital rates for minority groups.

4. We recommend that the Bureau of the Census and the National Center for Health Statistics conduct a birth registration and enumeration matching test in conjunction with the Census of 1970. The aims of this test should be to

    a. Test completeness of birth registration.

    b. Ascertain census underenumeration of the young.

    c. Determine quality of both birth registration and census data.

    d. Study differentials in infant mortality by characteristics in the family or household.

5.  We encourage the National Center for Health Statistics to work through the Public Health Conference on Records and Statistics and the American Association of Vital Registrars and Public Health Statisticians to ensure that a question concerning legitimacy will appear on the birth certificate and on the certificate of fetal death. This can be accomplished by having this item in the confidential section as recommended for the standard certificates* for 1968.

6.  We recommend that the National Center for Health Statistics encourage record linkage studies utilizing birth, fetal death, death, marriage, and divorce records. We recommend that the Bureau of the Census encourage record linkage studies based on the 1970 Census of Population and Housing.

7.  We encourage states to retain the question concerning race on the birth and death certificates, and we encourage states to include questions on race on marriage and divorce certificates. This can be accomplished by having this item in the confidential section as recommended for the standard certificates of 1968.

8.  We urge the National Center for Health Statistics to continue and expand studies of the completeness of death registration and studies of the quality of data obtained on death certificates.

9.  We urge the National Center for Health Statistics to encourage local agencies to classify birth and death certificates by city block or census tract, perhaps using the address register being developed by

---

*The standard certificate is that form which the National Center for Health Statistics recommends to the states as most appropriate.

the Bureau of the Census for the Census of 1970. This will make possible further studies of the vital rates of minority groups.

10. We support efforts to obtain a quinquennial census, and we recommend that such a census obtain adequate information to permit study of the vital rates of minority groups.

11. We urge states to affiliate as rapidly as possible with the Marriage and Divorce Registration Areas established by the National Center for Health Statistics.

12. We encourage the National Center for Health Statistics and the Bureau of the Census to explore, support, and conduct surveys of fertility expectations and performance. In particular, adequate information should be obtained for minority groups with distinctive fertility patterns.

## Needed Enlargement in Available Social Statistics for Negroes, Puerto Ricans, and Mexicans

1. The Conference recommends that the Census Bureau continue in the census to identify clearly Negroes, Puerto Ricans, Cubans, Mexicans, white persons of Spanish surname, and American Indians. For the specific groups for which more data are desired, Census publications should replace the categories of white and nonwhite with more specific ethnic or racial designations, for example, Negro, American Indian, and Cuban.

2. Federal statistical surveys should be designed from the beginning to provide data for specific minority groups. This may require

special sampling and tabulation programs in addition to specifications of content appropriate to the social situation of minorities.

3. The Bureau of the Census and other statistical agencies should continue to experiment with methods of identifying ethnic groups, for example, by ethnic origin, language spoken in the home, and birthplace of grandparents.

4. The presentation of survey and census results should be expanded in two ways—in summary form for general users and in easily available special tabulations for professional users.

5. The Conference recommends that the Census Bureau conduct frequent surveys to provide, for individual cities and the minority groups within cities, data of the type included in the program of the Current Population Survey.

6. A full census should be carried out more frequently than at present. A five-year census should replace the present ten-year census.

## Informing Organizations about the Census and Other Sources of Social Statistics

1. The Joint Center for Urban Studies of M.I.T. and Harvard should inform organizations interested in social statistics, particularly those concerned with minority groups, of the proceedings of this Conference.

# LIST OF CONFERENCE PARTICIPANTS

Mr. Sol Ackerman
Department of Housing and Urban
  Development
Washington, D. C.

Mr. Donald S. Akers
Staff Assistant
Population Division
Bureau of the Census
Washington, D. C.

Professor J. Herman Blake
Cowell College
University of California
Santa Cruz, Calif.

Mr. Lawrence N. Bloomberg
Assistant Chief for Social Sta-
  tistics
Office of Statistical Standards
U. S. Bureau of the Budget
Washington, D. C.

Miss Tobia Bressler
Chief, Ethnic Origins Statistics
  Branch
Bureau of the Census
Washington, D. C.

Professor Margaret Bright
School of Hygiene and Public
  Health
The Johns Hopkins University
Baltimore, Md.

Dr. Robert W. Buechley
Stanford Research Institute
Menlo Park, Calif.

Dr. Edgar Cahn
The Field Foundation
Washington, D. C.

Dr. James Cowhig, Chief
Cooperative Research and Demon-
  stration Grants Branch
Division of Research
Welfare Administration
Department of Health, Education,
  and Welfare
Washington, D. C.

Mr. James B. Crummett
Economic Development Unit
Department of Finance
City of Philadelphia, Pa.

Professor Otis Dudley Duncan
Department of Sociology
University of Michigan
Ann Arbor, Mich.

Mr. James Dyer
National Urban League
New York, N. Y.

Dr. Albert Ross Eckler, Director
U. S. Bureau of the Census
Washington, D. C.

Professor G. Franklin Edwards
Department of Sociology
Howard University
Washington, D. C.

Professor Reynolds Farley
Department of Sociology
Duke University
Durham, N. C.

Mr. John Feild, Director
Community Relations Service
U. S. Conference of Mayors
Washington, D. C.

Mr. Verrick O. French
The Washington Center for Metro-
    politan Studies
Washington, D. C.

Dr. Paul C. Glick
Assistant Chief
Population Division
U. S. Bureau of the Census
Washington, D. C.

Mr. Paul M. Grams
Joint Center for Urban Studies of
    M.I.T. and Harvard University
Cambridge, Mass.

Professor Bernard G. Greenberg
Chairman
Department of Biostatistics
School of Public Health
University of North Carolina
Chapel Hill, N. C.

Mrs. Eunice Grier
Research Director
U. S. Commission on Civil Rights
Washington, D. C.

Dr. Robert Grove, Chief
Division of Vital Statistics
U. S. Public Health Service
Department of Health, Education,
    and Welfare
Washington, D. C.

Miss Joyce Haney
Joint Center for Urban Studies of
    M.I.T. and Harvard University
Cambridge, Mass.

Mrs. Sara S. Hartman
Director of Research
Baltimore Urban Renewal and
    Housing Agency
Baltimore, Md.

Dr. Robert G. Hayden
National Conference on the Prob-
    lems of the Mexican American
    and Puerto Rican Communities
Washington, D. C.

Professor David M. Heer
Harvard School of Public Health
Boston, Mass.

Dr. Earl E. Huyck
Program Analysis Officer
Office of the Secretary
U. S. Department of Health, Edu-
    cation, and Welfare
Washington, D. C.

Mrs. Hilda M. James, Deputy
    Director
Relocation Staff, Office of Com-
    munity Development
Department of Housing and Urban
    Development
Washington, D. C.

Mr. Harold Kempner, Coordinator
Mayor's Committee for Human Re-
    sources Development
City of Detroit, Mich.

Professor Everett S. Lee, Chairman
Department of Sociology and
    Anthropology
University of Massachusetts
Amherst, Mass.

Dr. Hylan Lewis
Professor of Sociology
Howard University
Washington, D. C.
        and
Fellow, Metropolitan Applied Re-
    search Center
New York, N. Y.

Dr. Forrest E. Linder, Director
National Center for Health Sta-
    tistics
Public Health Service
Department of Health, Education,
    and Welfare
Washington, D. C.

Dr. Michael Marien
Syracuse University
Syracuse, N. Y.

Miss Margaret Martin
Office of Statistical Standards
U. S. Bureau of the Budget
Washington, D. C.

Dr. Herman P. Miller, Chief
Population Division
U. S. Bureau of the Census
Washington, D. C.

Dr. Joseph Monserrat, Director
Commonwealth of Puerto Rico
Migration Division, Department
    of Labor
New York, N. Y.

Professor Daniel P. Moynihan,
    Director
Joint Center for Urban Studies of
    M.I.T. and Harvard University
Cambridge, Mass.

Mrs. Dorothy Newman
Bureau of Labor Statistics
U. S. Department of Labor
Washington, D. C.

Dr. John Norton
George Washington University
Washington, D. C.

Mr. David Norman, Chief
Appeals and Research Section
Civil Rights Division
U. S. Department of Justice
Washington, D. C.

Mr. Joseph Oberman, Chief
Economic Development Unit
Department of Finance
City of Philadelphia, Pa.

Professor Daniel Price
Department of Sociology
University of Texas
Austin, Texas

Mr. Leon Pritzker, Chief
Response Research Branch
U. S. Bureau of the Census
Washington, D. C.

Mr. Robert A. Reveles
Special Assistant to Rep. Morris
    K. Udall
House Office Building
Washington, D. C.

Mr. Edward Ray Rickman
Aide to Congressman Diggs
House of Representatives
Washington, D. C.

Mr. James K. Rocks
Department of Health, Education,
    and Welfare
Office of Education
Washington, D. C.

Mrs. Naomi D. Rothwell
Response Research Branch
U. S. Bureau of the Census
Washington, D. C.

Dr. Henry D. Sheldon
Population Division
U. S. Bureau of the Census
Washington, D. C.

Mr. Jacob Siegel
Staff Assistant
Population Division
U. S. Bureau of the Census
Washington, D. C.

Dr. Mortimer Spiegelman
American Public Health Association
New York, N. Y.

Mr. Robert Stein
Work Patterns Analyses
Division of Program and Long Range
    Research Studies
Office of Research and Statistics
Social Security Administration
Washington, D. C.

Dr. Conrad Taeuber
Assistant Director for Demographic
    Fields
U. S. Bureau of the Census
Washington, D. C.

Professor Karl E. Taeuber
Department of Sociology
University of Wisconsin
Madison, Wisc.

Mr. William L. Taylor
Staff Director
U. S. Commission on Civil Rights
Washington, D. C.

Mr. Joseph Waksberg
U. S. Bureau of the Census
Washington, D. C.

Mr. Louis Winnick
The Ford Foundation
New York, N. Y.

Mr. William K. Wolfe, Executive
    Director
United Community Corporation
Newark, N. J.